D1478867

WOMEN'S MYSTERIES

WOMEN'S MYSTERIES

Toward a Poetics of Gender

Christine Downing

CROSSROAD • NEW YORK

1992

The Crossroad Publishing Company
370 Lexington Avenue, New York, NY 10017

Printed in the United States of America

Library of Congress Cataloging-in-Publication Data

Downing, Christine, 1931–
    Women's mysteries : towards a poetics of gender / Christine Downing.
    p. cm.
    Includes bibliographical references.
    ISBN 0-8245-1197-2 (cloth)
    1. Femininity (Psychology) 2. Women—Psychology. 3. Sex differences
(Psychology) 4. Feminist psychology.   I. Title.
BF175.5.F45D69   1992
155.3'33—dc20   92-17501
                                                                    CIP

Grateful acknowledgment is made to the following persons and publishers for permission to quote from published material:

Meridel LeSueur: for lines from "Rites of Ancient Ripening," from *Ripening* by Meridel LeSueur. Old Westbury: The Feminist Press, 1982. Reprinted by permission of the author.

Kathlee Miller: for lines from "Mysteries," from *Venus Rising* 2, no. 6 (Sept./Oct. 1988), Santa Barbara, Calif. Reprinted by permission of the author.

Eileen Moeller: for lines from 'ten years ago." Reprinted by permission of the author.

William L. Rukeyser: from lines from "Myth" © Muriel Rukeyser, by permission of William L. Rukeyser, from *Out of Silence*. New York: Tri-Quarterly Press, 1992.

Alma Luz Villaneuva: for lines from "Sisters," from *Bloodroot* by Alma Luz Villanueva. Copyright 1977, 1985 by Alma Luz Villanueva. Reprinted by permission of Place of Herons Press and the author.

Bloodaxe Books: for lines from "The Way Towards Each Other" by Jeni Couzyn, from *Life by Drowning: Selected Poems* by Jeni Couzyn. Bloodaxe Books, 1985. Reprinted by permission of Bloodaxe Books.

Houghton Mifflin Company: for lines from *Duino Elegies and the Sonnets to Orpheus* by Rainer Maria Rilke, translated by A. Poulin, Jr. Reprinted by permission of Houghton Mifflin Company.

New Directions: for lines from "Beginners" by Denise Levertov, from *Candles in Babylon* by Denise Levertov. Copyright © 1982 by Denise Levertov. Reprinted by permission of New Directions Publishing Corp.

New Directions: for lines from "Asphodel, That Greeny Flower" by William Carlos Williams, from *The Collected Poems of William Carlos Williams, Vol. II, 1939–1962*. Copyright © 1962 by William Carlos Williams. Reprinted by permission of New Directions Publishing Corp.

W. W. Norton & Company: for lines from "Now I Become Myself" by May Sarton, from *Collected Poems (1930–1973)* by May Sarton. Copyright © 1974 by May Sarton. Reprinted by permission of W. W. Norton & Company, Inc.

Random House: for lines from "Brooding" by Eugenio Montale, from *Otherwise* by Eugenio Montale, translated by Jonathan Galassi. Translation copyright © 1984 by Jonathan Galassi. Reprinted by permission of Random House, Inc.

Random House: for lines from "The Moment" by Sharon Olds, from *The Dead and the Living* by Sharon Olds. Copyright © 1983 by Sharon Olds, Reprinted by permission of Alfred A. Knopf, Inc.

Random House: for lines from "Something to Look Forward To" by Marge Piercy, from *Available Light* by Marge Piercy. Copyright © 1988 by Middlemarch, Inc. Reprinted by permission of Alfred A. Knopf, Inc.

Random House: for lines from "Unlearning to Not Speak" by Marge Piercy, from *Circles on the Water* by Marge Piercy. Copyright © 1982 by Marge Piercy. Reprinted by permission of Alfred A. Knopf, Inc.

Oxford University Press: for lines from "An Indian Pregnancy Song," from *Folksongs of the Maikal Hills*, edited by V. Elwin and S. Hilvale. Oxford University Press, 1944. Reprinted by permission of Oxford University Press, New Delhi.

BOA Editions: for lines from "The Lost Baby Poem" copyright © 1987 by Lucille Clifton. Reprinted from *Good Women: Poems and a Memoir, 1969–1980* by Lucille Clifton. Reprinted by permission of BOA Editions, Ltd., 92 Park Avenue, Brockport, N.Y. 14420.

This book is written in honor of Esther Harding who died some twenty years ago

and as a sixtieth birthday present to myself.

Contents

List of Illustrations

1. M. Esther Harding, photograph taken by Edwin Gann Snyder. Used with permission of the C. G. Jung Foundation for Analytical Psychology, New York.

2. Relief depicting two girls in a ritual dance, from the metope of the temple of Hera at Paestum. Courtesy of Hirmer Verlag, Munich.

3. Vase painting depicting a maenad, the "Brygos Schale." Used with permission of the Staatliche Antikensammlungen und Glyptothek, Munich.

4. Head of the "Kore with the pensive face," Acropolis Museum in Athens. Used with permission of the Hellenic Republic Ministry of Culture.

5. Archaic statue of the Sphinx from Sparta, now at the National Museum in Athens. Used with permission of the Hellenic Republic Ministry of Culture.

6. Relief of the lion-headed Sekhmet, Temple of Karnak in Egypt. Mansell Collection.

Acknowledgments

The decision to write this book came, not from dreams as has been true for most of my other books, but during a sleepless night, the last night of a sabbatical year. I spent the year catching up with myself and with my friends, taking time to enjoy being with the woman I love and to delight in the beautiful surroundings of our home and the nearby beach, revisiting Germany, the country where I was born, and Greece, the land which my soul seems to recognize as home. It was a year of many momentous changes in the outer world, most importantly for me, the ending of the division between East and West Germany which meant that, for the first time since I left Leipzig when I was four, I could freely return not just to the country but to the *land* of my birth.

Inwardly, less seemed to have happened during that year, but as I lay awake, I felt myself not restless but full of energy or, rather, of energies, energies which seemed to originate from many points without and within my body and to be converging in my womb. I felt a conception happen: the conception of this book. For as I continued to attend to this sensuous experience, I had a vivid realization of how themes and questions that had occupied me during the last few years (some of which had issued in talks or papers or workshops) and that I had thought of as discrete and unconnected all really belonged together and needed to be brought together. Separately they meant less than they would mean in juxtaposition; but when conjoined, each would need to be reworked, recreated. The project felt urgent; turning to it has, indeed, entailed interrupting work on another project already begun: a study of the mythological representation of descents to the underworld and their relevance to our "life-stopping" experiences. Now that this book is done, I can again honor the pull to return to that underworld.

As I think back upon the many who have helped me toward this book, I am struck by how many of them are men, men who in a sense have been asking me Freud's question "What do women want?" with a new urgency, as though to have some better understanding of women were essential to their knowledge of themselves. This realization makes it even more evident to me than it had been earlier that, though this book is focused explicitly on aspects of female experience, it is written for men as well as for women.

I want to thank:

River Malcolm for lying beside me the night in Bermuda during which I dreamt up this book and for bearing with me through all the days of its writing.

Patricia Finley for going to hear Esther Harding with me one spring evening more than thirty years ago and for remaining true ever since to the life direction we glimpsed then.

Stan Passy and Steve Aizenstat of Pacifica Graduate School for inviting me to speak at a conference on "Reconciling the Differences" and thus encouraging me to try to articulate how complexly body and soul are intertwined in the psychology of women.

Merida Wexler for her honest and courageous exploration of the travails and joys of female embodiment.

Harry Buck and Nancy Corson Carter for asking me to write an article on the Crone for the fifteenth anniversary issue of *Anima*.

Richard Hycner and Maurice Friedman for asking me to speak to the San Diego Dialogical Psychotherapy Institute on my approach to revisioning the psychology of women.

Karen Brown, Carol Christ, Adria Evans, Jan Clanton Collins, Eleanor Garner, Puanani Harvey, Sandra Downing, Delores Jacobs, Kelley O'Neel, Suzanne Harding, Jean Thomson, and Sabine Scheffler for conversations, some recent, some long ago, which have deeply affected my own understanding of women.

Frank Oveis and George Lawler, my editors at Crossroad/Continuum: Frank for his immediate enthusiastic response to the manuscript; George (whose midwiving skills I have acknowledged before) for recognizing that I had conceived not one book but two, this one and its fraternal twin, *Gods in Our Midst*.

And, Elaine Rother who as Elaine Estwick has appeared in the acknowledgments of all my earlier books and who remains *the* Elaine without whose generously extended help and modestly garbed competence none of them could have been brought to completion.

·1·

INITIATION
A TRIBUTE TO
ESTHER HARDING

T he only time I met Esther Harding, more than thirty years ago, she was ten years older than I am now. She had been invited to a nearby university to speak on *Journey Into Self*, her book-length exploration of Bunyan's *Pilgrim's Progress*. A woman friend and I who had been reading Jung together and beginning to help one another attend to our dreams (and who had wrestled, not too successfully, with Harding's study of Jungian theory, *Psychic Energy*) went together. I remember very little of what Esther Harding said that evening but the impression she made on me has remained indelible. Here was a *woman*, not a nurturing mother nor a sexual playmate but a woman who clearly had her center in herself. She was as strong, as intelligent, as direct, as the spinster headmistress of my youth, her face as life-marked as that of the women in Grant Wood's portraits, but she conveyed a liveliness, an unquenched curiosity, a wisdom of soul, I had never found in those figures. My friend and I went home together and sitting over coffee in her kitchen, we discovered that somehow in Esther Harding's presence each of us had come to a life-shaping decision. "I am going into therapy," my friend said. "I want to become an analyst." "I am going to graduate school," I said. "I want to be a teacher." And so it has been.

Of all her books, *Woman's Mysteries* (which I must have read for the first time soon after hearing her speak) is the one that best communicates the insights and the power we were brought into touch with that evening. Although it was written almost sixty years ago, it was out of print for a long time, and only since its appearance as a paperback in the mid 1970s has the book achieved much popular recognition. It undoubtedly meant something different to the women who discovered it then during the early years of the contemporary wave of feminism than it had to those who read it when it first appeared, and, of course, means something different still to those of us who discover or return to it now.

When I reread it just as I was beginning that engagement with the goddesses of ancient Greece which eventually issued in my book *The Goddess,* I felt the book was directly addressed to me and to my contemporaries. Jung often remarked that his psychology was most appropriate to patients in the second half of life whose outwardly successful lives had become meaningless to them. Somewhat analogously *Woman's Mysteries* seemed newly relevant at a stage in the history of the women's movement when many of us were finding that after outward success in the realms of family or work or both, after a period of identifying ourselves in terms of familial relationships and/or professional achievement, other questions about what it means to be a woman had begun to appear. What had earlier given energy and direction to our lives had lost the power to do so.

Harding's book seemed a still unique attempt to name what is distinctive about the psychology of women: unique because it is neither "feminist" in the then popular sense of asserting that women can and should be just as "masculine" as men nor "feminine" in the sense of supporting what we had come to decry as "the feminine mystique." Harding introduces a perspective not ordered to our conscious versions of our self nor directly focused on the social roles we choose or feel forced to play.

She suggests that knowing what it means to be a woman is not as simple as might at first appear, that if we are honest we will recognize that we are in some ways a mystery to ourselves and not only to men. She invites us to *attend* to this mystery, and thus to serve the soul as the *therapeutes* of the ancient world served the gods to whom they were dedicated.

Harding reminds us how much of the psychology about women has come from men who call to us beguilingly: Be our souls, our mothers, our muses. Comfort us, nurture us, inspire us, seduce us. Provide us with an excuse for our failures. Teach us how to feel, to relate, to listen to our intuitions.

These are visions of woman which spring from men's needs, from their sense of incompleteness, visions which see woman as the other, the opposite, the complementary. Harding sees how all too easy it is for women to be pulled into this logic, either by accepting it (and playing the role of a man's anima) or by saying, No, that's not what we're like. We're just like you. Because the second alternative often seems the more attractive (since the so-called feminine attributes have all, even if in subtle ways, been made into inferior ones and are less adaptive to achievement in the "masculine" world), many women in her time and still today join the "flight from the feminine" which pervades our culture. But Harding was persuaded that though our egos may thus come to have a "masculine" cast, our souls (like the souls of men, she would say) are "feminine." Women, like men, she asserts, need to develop both their "masculine" and "feminine" aspects and, luckily, may be more likely to discover this need than men—because less likely to find another who will carry the "feminine" side for them.

This seemed so freshly pertinent to many of us in the seventies that it was stunning to realize that in the thirties Harding was already addressing "liberated" women who had discovered something barren and arid in their way of being in the world, but was *not* calling them back to traditional feminine roles nor to a stereotypical feminine psychological orientation. She was instead affirming the possibility of achieving an androgynous consciousness—by which she meant not a desexualized consciousness but one in which the "masculine" and the "feminine" would be fruitfully related, as in a sacred marriage, a *hieros gamos.*

Of course the androgynous ideal had already been put forward by Harding's mentor, Carl Jung, but Jung tends to see this ideal as primarily applicable to men, whom he encourages to integrate their anima (his name for their unconscious contrasexual "feminine" aspect). Women in touch with their animus (their "masculine" side) he saw as likely to be animus-*possessed,* unhappy and unattractive. Jung often writes as though he believes that women should stay "feminine" in order to help men access their own "feminine" potential and almost always assumes that their ego orientation will be a "feminine" one.[1]

Without ever directly challenging Jungian theory, Harding actually puts forward a radically different understanding, one which foreshadows Irene Claremont de Castillejo's realization that the "soul image" of women is feminine not masculine[2] and James Hillman's attempt to disconnect anima/animus from contrasexuality.[3] The conscious ego orientation of both men and women, Harding says, may be "masculine," that is, dominated by the thinking function and by goal orientation, and both men and women may need to struggle to access their more undeveloped and unknown "feminine" potential, their anima. That is, Harding recognizes the problematics of modern women's relationship to the "feminine":

> They cannot resume the feminine values in the old instinctive
> and unconscious way. . . . If they are to get in touch with their
> lost feminine side it must be by the hard road of a conscious
> adaptation.[4]

Yet she believes that in some way this process is different for women than for men, that our pull to our lost feminine soul has a different quality than men's pull toward the anima, for we experience the encounter with the anima as the rediscovery of what is already ourself rather than as the discovery of an unknown "other" within.

I remember how right and how liberating this felt when I first read it. It was one of those occasions when someone had *said* what I already *knew,* but only half-knew I knew and had had no words for. My friend and I had begun working on our dreams together precisely in order to get in touch with what we haltingly called "soul," "depth," "creativity," but which we knew to be essential to our wholeness as women. Though both of us at that period in our lives felt fulfilled as sexual beings and as mothers, we knew something was missing. Thus in my midtwenties I gratefully agreed with Harding, Yes, it is my more "feminine" side that I am out of touch with, that I need to learn how to access and love and live from. Yes, it is my anima I'm longing to connect with, not my animus, whatever that is. Yes, that anima aspect is in some sense the *real* me from which I somehow got separated.

Now, her words no longer satisfy me—but I might never have come to my own without their help. I can no longer use "masculine" or "feminine" with the assurance that she takes for granted. Indeed, I cannot use these terms without putting quotation marks around them, even when I am trying to recapitulate what she says. I have become uncomfortable with the very notions of "anima" and "animus." I am no longer satisfied with "androgyny" as a helpful way of imaging human wholeness, for women or for men. I am suspicious of understandings of "the archetypal" that presuppose the existence of universal essences. I cringe at Harding's use of "primitive," and at her speaking of young women of marriageable age as "girls." I would say—will say—so much differently from the way she says it, and yet at some more important level I sense that what I most want to say now is really not that different from what she said in language that grew out of and spoke to her time.

Harding says that a woman's development of an androgynous consciousness depends on her being able to differentiate and give value to the "feminine" in herself. She sees the age-old images of the feminine contained in ancient myths and rituals and the images of our own dreams as an invaluable resource for bringing into our consciousness a knowledge of the feminine which we will recognize as in some sense already deeply familiar.

I am still amazed by how clearly Harding recognized that a truly "feminine" psychology would have a different form and not just a different subject from the "masculine" psychologies which were then the only available models. She takes care to say that she is proposing a psychology composed from a "feminine" perspective, but that this does not mean a psychology pertinent only to women.

The in-one-self-ness, the freedom from definition through relationships, which the book celebrates, points to a psychology that starts from within-ness, from introversion and thus from the imagination. Such a psychology begins by recognizing that its knowledge emerges from the psyche's self-reflections, reflections which appear as images rather than as ideas.

> No attempt has been made to discuss the matter from a purely intellectual standpoint, but instead it is presented in the form in which it is actually experienced by modern woman, as well as by her more primitive and less rationally developed sisters. The material taken for consideration and psychological interpretation has been gleaned from ancient and primitive sources and from the dreams and phantasies of modern people and presents its subject as parable or allegory, not as rationally established fact.[5]

Though she never used the phrase, from my first reading I understood Harding to be proposing that we replace *psycho-logic,* psychological theory as it has been promulgated until now, with a *psycho-poetics.*

That the psyche can best be described through a poetics was later reaffirmed by Marie Louise von Franz in her *Problems of the Feminine in Fairytales* (based on lectures given in 1958–59) and by de Castillejo in *Knowing Woman* (1973). All three women recognize the hunger of women for images through which we might see *ourselves,* for goddesses not as objects of worship but as figures through whom we might discover the varied archetypal aspects of the feminine. These women understood themselves as initiating a process whereby women would nourish one another through the sharing of such images.

At times I regret the reluctance of these women of an earlier generation to risk theoretical wrestling with "father" Jung and see their decision to emphasize "images" rather than "ideas" as betraying a perhaps unconscious conviction that theorizing is a male perogative. Yet I also see how right they were in recognizing that the psyche needs images to nurture its growth. For images provide a knowledge that we can interiorize rather than apply, and take deep into ourselves to that place where, as Laurens van der Post once put it, the reeds and grasses grow. Certainly, I have been immeasurably nourished not only by the images which have emerged out of my own dreams but by those which have been entrusted to me by other women, by friends like Carol Christ or Karen Brown or by contemporaries of mine whom I know only through their writing such as Adrienne Rich or Audre Lorde. And, as Harding says, the myths and cultic traditions of earlier times serve to provide confirmation of the significance of our contemporary dreams and fantasy images as well as help us to gain a richer sense of their implications:

> These accumulations represent the wisdom of antique and primitive men who were nearer to nature than ourselves. They may hold treasures of understanding for us, or, on the other hand, they may be merely archaeological curiosities. We cannot take them uncritically as representing a wisdom appropriate for us, as well as the ancients, but neither can we discard them as valueless merely because they are old.[6]

Harding called her book *Woman's Mysteries*, in part to draw the attention of modern women to the mysteriousness of their own femininity, but also to refer to the secret female initiation rites of the ancient Near Eastern world. She understands the "secret" of these Mysteries to have been the knowledge that "the gods are not beings external to man but are rather psychological forces or principles which have been projected and personified in the gods."[7] All through her book Harding seeks to open us to the still potent psychological significance of ancient rites and myths.

Indeed, her book is itself an initiation into these mysteries. She lays particular emphasis on the cult of the moon goddess, since the moon is "the symbol which above all others has stood throughout the ages for that in woman which is distinctively feminine."[8] She shows us how for the mythic imagination the moon's cyclical changes connect it to women's monthly physiological cycle and to the psychological counterparts of that cycle. To apprehend the significance of this analogical rather than causal correspondence is, Harding suggests, to be freed from the blinders of a literalizing, "masculine" objectivity and to be introduced to a more poetic, a more authentically "feminine" mode of consciousness.

Reminding us of how almost universally in primitive cultures women are isolated and deemed taboo during their menstrual cycles, Harding affirms the psychological significance of these times of withdrawal which she believes may often have been *chosen* by women rather than forced upon them. She suggests that the days spent alone or with other women may often be the nearest equivalent for women of male initiation ceremonies which involve their participants in an arduous solitary ordeal:

> The women do not go into a similar seclusion for a single initiation experience, but every month they must go apart for a few days and remain alone, in close touch with that instinctual force which dominates them from within. . . . It is probable that the contact which women obtain with the deeper trends of the unconscious at this monthly retreat is less formulated, less articulate, than is the case with men.[9]

The young women's initiation was less focused on a single transformative event; the wisdom it yielded was more diffuse and often remained more subliminal. Harding hopes to help women of our time recover this wisdom and bring it to a more articulate consciousness than it may ever have had in earlier times.

She notes that, because we no longer regard menstruating women as unclean or sick, we may be encouraged to disregard changes of mood and psychic orientation which we may nonetheless still feel. She wants to persuade us to recognize that women still need times of withdrawal from men and from their "masculine" side. She encourages us to become more attentive to our shifting moods and thus to open ourselves to the different self-knowledge that might come from asking, What do these feelings mean?

> The woman also has an opportunity at the dark of the moon to get into touch with a deeper and more fundamental layer of her own psychic life. . . . An inner necessity is calling her to introvert, to withdraw psychologically from the demands of her external life and live for a little while in the secret places of her own heart.[10]

Harding further observed that a "lunar" psychology such as the one she imagines women constructing would yield a different understanding of individuation, of psychological integration, than that proposed by the masculine "solar" psychological theories which were the only theories available at the time she was writing. To look upon the moon as the most compelling image of the self leads to a recognition of the self as changeable and many-faced. It means accepting disharmony, inertia, restlessness, decay, even madness and death, as experiences to be lived rather than as problems to be overcome.

Most significantly, Harding reminds us that "to the Greeks the power of the moon was represented by Hecate, the Dark Moon":

> The Moon Goddess is not only Goddess of Storms and of Fertility, that is of all disturbances and creations in the outer world, she is also goddess of disturbances and creative activity which take place in the inner world. She is responsible for lunacy and, on the positive side, is Giver of Vision.[11]

It is what happens in the depths, in the unconscious, in the underworld, that is truly transformative. Once again, Harding highlights the importance of the mysterious, the unknown, the hidden.

Harding's most focused expositions of the significance of the moon goddesses come in chapters which present fascinatingly detailed readings of the various versions of the myths and cultic traditions surrounding Ishtar and Isis. Even now each time I pick up the book another episode, another image, lights up for me, evokes my own further amplification and suggests a new way of viewing some moment of my own history. It was when I first read this book that I glimpsed how attending to all the different animals and talismans, relationships and adventures, which cluster about a particular divinity might open us to a new vision of our own multiform identity. It seems not at all accidental that I initially returned to the book at just the time when I found myself led by a dream to go in search of Persephone, the Greek goddess of the underworld. I was then for the first time having direct experience of how personally transformative focused engagement with an ancient goddess tradition can be. Thus on that rereading I often found myself murmuring, Yes. Yes, I know.

On every rereading I have found that the passages in the book which most move me are those devoted to the virgin goddess who is one-in-herself. Virginity, as Harding comes to understand it, means not a lack of sexual experience, not an intact hymen, but, quite simply, not being married. She tells us that in many early cultures a young unmarried woman was understood not as her father's property but rather as her own mistress. "A girl belongs to *herself* while she is virgin—unwed—and may not be compelled either to maintain chastity or to yield to an unwanted embrace":

> It is in this sense that the moon goddesses may rightly be called virgin. The quality of virginity is, indeed, characteristic of them. Other goddesses of ancient and primitive religions do not partake of it: they are not one-in-themselves. They have apparently no separate existence of their own, but are conceived of only as the wives or counterparts of the gods from whom they derive both their power and their prestige. . . .
>
> The relation of the Moon Mother to the god associated with her is entirely different. She is goddess of sexual love but not of marriage. There is no male god who as husband rules her conduct or determines her qualities. Instead, she is the mother of a son, whom she controls. When he grows up he becomes her lover and then dies, only to be born again as her son. The Moon Goddess belongs to a matriarchal, not to a patriarchal, system. She is not related to any god as wife or "counterpart." She is her own mistress, virgin, one-in-herself.[12]

Extrapolating from this understanding of virginity, Harding suggests that we might call any woman, whether married or not, virgin, if she, too, has her center in herself. Any woman who does not do what she does to please or attract or win another, or to gain another's interest or approval or love, and who is not dependent on what others think is in this sense a virgin—whereas a woman who is dependent, even if only on some idea of how she "ought" to behave, is not.

I continue to find Harding's reinterpretation of virginity invaluable in showing us that what matters is not our marital status but whether we feel ourselves *defined* by our relationships. I have also come to understand that, though some of us (like Aphrodite) may maintain our virginity effortlessly, others (more like Artemis) will find ourselves continually engaged in defending it—and some of us (like Hera) may discover that a lost virginity can be recovered in later life.

This image of the virgin goddess not dependent for her sense of her own identity on father or husband or son (or, I would add, on mother or female partner or daughter), this vision of a female finding her self *in herself* is what continues to pull me back to this book—even though today I would not polarize autonomy and relatedness in the way Harding did, and may have needed to in her own life. For I sense that without ever being directly autobiographical, *Woman's Mysteries* is a very personal testimony. I know that whenever I read Harding's moving invocation of in-one-selfness, I cannot help but recall the impact of her presence at Drew University those many years ago.

·2·

RITES OF INCORPORATION

I n the ancient world women were ritually initiated by other women into womanhood through participation in women's mysteries. Almost everything I've written in the last fifteen years represents an attempt to revive and reanimate such mysteries—to honor the mysteriousness of women not only to men but to women and to reconnect us to those sacred myths and rituals of initiation through which women of the ancient world were taught who they were. Participation in these cultic activities helped them discover and become themselves; remembrance of these traditions may help us do likewise.

Such tales and rites remind us that our femaleness is not simply a biological given, but rather shaped through acts of social, psychological, and religious interpretation. Of course the values and perspectives some of us have rediscovered (or found confirmed) by attending to these ancient mysteries are just as much human creations as those central to the patriarchal systems we contest. The matristic perspective is neither ontologically grounded nor inherently normative. Validating it does not entail dismissing all other symbols and beliefs as false or worthless. I do, however, see aspects of this perspective as profoundly relevant to the urgencies of our present historical moment— relevant not only to women but to all humans.

I believe that we need to learn all we possibly can about these alternative wisdoms, to listen to the for so long denigrated sources and to resay what we hear in ways that might make this wisdom effective in our world before it is too late. Let me be clear: I am not saying that if we do this, the continuance of life on this earth will be assured, the renewal of earth established. As the last chapter of this book will make evident, I do not have that kind of trusting faith. Nonetheless, I believe it matters terribly that we do all we can, that we try to block out all that distracts us from this task and join in creating a ritual space dedicated to learning what we can from the matristic past, from our bodies, from one another.

Speaking Among Ourselves

The ancient "mysteries" were secret rites which revealed hidden dimensions of experience, dimensions not to be named in profane contexts.

Men were excluded and those who violated the taboo suffered severe consequences. Legends attest that men who sought to enter Demeter's temple during the rites associated with the Thesmophoria were castrated, and in the *Bacchae* Pentheus is killed and dismembered for spying upon the maenads' celebrations. Yet the matrons who temporarily left their households to participate in the Demetrian rite or to join the maenads on the hilltops later returned to those with whom they shared their everyday lives. Thus there is a sense in which those who were left behind and who welcomed the celebrants' return were also part of the ritual community, albeit not as active participants.

I understand myself as writing within a ritually defined sacred space—as one woman speaking of her experience to other women. In my imagination I find myself in the center of a clearing with the other women of my tribe performing our sacred rites—aware that at least some of the men of the tribe stand at the edge of the clearing; they know they may not interfere but are also assured that they have a place there at the periphery. Later, there may be another rite, a ritual of incorporation which would include them as active participants—but that ritual will only become possible if this one is allowed to proceed uninterrupted.

This image is very vivid to me; it carries the authority of a recurrent dream image, though as far as I can remember it has never actually appeared in a dream. I do, however, recall a dream I had in my early twenties, actually the first dream I ever took the trouble of writing down, which may be the basis of the image. In that dream I stood at the edge of a forest clearing on a moonlit night with the other young maidens of my tribe watching the men of our people engage in the ritual installation of a young man as our new chief. At the climax of the ceremony this youth came over to where we stood, singled me out and drew me into the center. Then, as the rite continued, I as his chosen bride became a performer in the dance. Later, on the basis of this ritual empowerment, I was able to take on a solitary heroic role which ensured the survival of my people at a time of great threat. I understand this dream as suggesting that then, forty years ago, it seemed that entry into the men's circle would help a woman discover herself, but I know that in more recent decades it has at last again become *our* time to dance our own dance.

I believe that it has been imperative not to be seduced into explaining ourselves to men but rather faithfully to dedicate ourselves to sharing with one another what we know and don't know, what we fear and hope, remember and imagine. I am struck by how several times when I have taught classes on goddesses or on the psychology of women, the few men taking the class have chosen to sit on the sidelines and listen. Afterwards they have confided how transformative this access to women's ways of being with one another has been. Because they had deliberately chosen not to violate what they recognized as a *temenos*, a sacred space, we women had truly been able to speak among ourselves as though they were not there.

Thus as I try to articulate a psychology of women that begins with female experience and that honors the diversity among us, I know I don't want to speak to men, nor to speak of how we are different from them. I would like as far as possible to escape formulations given their shape by the myth of difference, by the fantasy of opposites. We all know the litany:

> *Where is she?*
> *Activity/passivity*
> *Sun/Moon*
> *Culture/Nature*
> *Day/Night*
>
> *Father/Mother*
> *Head/Heart*
> *Intelligible/Palpable*
> *Logos/Pathos Form, convex, step, advance, semen,*
> *progress.*
> *Matter, concave, ground—where steps are taken,*
> *holding- and dumping-ground.*
> *Man*
> *Woman*

> Always the same metaphor: we follow it, it carries us, beneath all its figure, where discourse is organized. If we read or speak, the same thread or double braid is leading us throughout literature, philosophy, criticism, centuries of representation and reflection.[1]

Of course it is not easy to avoid speaking of female experience in terms of how it is like or unlike that of men or letting the shape of the discourse be defined by what men have said about themselves or us—so that we respond by correcting here or there or by rejecting. It is not easy, but I believe it is necessary and possible. Like Rainer Maria Rilke I imagine that

> Someday there will be girls and women whose name will no longer mean the mere opposite of the male, but something in itself, something that makes one think not of any complement and limit, but only of life and reality: the female human being.[2]

I have learned that I must speak of *women's* mysteries, rather than of *woman's* mysteries as Esther Harding did, for I cannot comfortably share her assumption that there is some essence of the feminine, of woman, some female archetype, in which we all participate. Today we easily recognize the limitations of such essentialism and of the normative and hierarchical assumptions it often masks. (Not that these hierarchical assumptions are always denigrating and misogynist. There is also a feminist version of essentialism, one which endorses the notion of a romantically idealized female essence miraculously untainted despite its having been obscured through millennia of patriarchal oppression. Thus to view "patriarchy" as a universal always-the-same oppressive institution is itself a mode of essentialism which effaces historical differences and erases other axes of oppression.)[3]

Of course I recognize that just substituting the plural "women" for Harding's "woman" does not really suffice to dispose of essentialism. In fact, extricating oneself from its assumptions is more difficult than we might at first imagine. Already ten years ago, although the title of my book on Greek goddesses (*The Goddess: Mythological Images of the Feminine*) might suggest otherwise, I saw myself as articulating a richly plural, polytheistic, understanding of women. Nevertheless, I think now that I failed fully to realize then that for many women who do not share my lifelong intimacy with Greek mythology, what I wrote seemed ethnocentric and elitist. I have since come to understand more fully how easily the theorizing of articulate, academic, privileged women like myself may become the "default position" which presents the perspectives of other women as variations on, modifications of, or additions to ours, and how easily and unconsciously we may put forward a presumptively normative vision analogous to the masculine one we so forcefully critique. As Elizabeth Spelman has shown, simply acknowledging the theoretical importance of inclusion without doing the work of actually including the other voices is also suspect. How easy it is to allow imagination to replace perception and thus grant ourselves the illusion of listening and learning without its real risks and pains.

> Essentialism invites me to take what I understand to be true of me "as a woman" for some golden nugget of womanness all women have as women, and it makes the participation of other women inessential to the production of the story. How lovely: the many turn out to be one, and the one they are is me.[4]

I see now that I must question not only the myth of difference but also the myth of identity, must acknowledge the always problematic relation between Woman and women, between woman and feminist, women and the feminine, and keep in mind the salience of other axes of differentiation, especially race and class.

There is a sense, I have come to recognize, in which the feminist "we" is always a fantasy, though I continue to believe it may also serve valid purposes. I know I have become self-conscious about using this "we," and then nonetheless fall into using it without noticing—until I reread and then question what I have written.

I note how changeable this "we" as I use it is and how often indefinite; sometimes I seem implicitly to include all humans, sometimes all women, sometimes other feminists, or perhaps other female theorists or other post-Jungians. I see that I sometimes seem to be inclusive where I have no right to be, or to be exclusive in ways I don't quite mean. I know I don't mean to use the "we" imperiously, to coerce community or presume agreement when it doesn't exist—yet I find myself unwilling to write in the third person or always in the singular. I am unwilling to be rendered mute or isolate. I mean to speak not *for* but *to* and *among*.

I imagine a *poetics* of feminism. What my "we" intends to express is not an assumption of identity but a longing for a community. For I see the image of a community of women as a fiction, a myth. I hope for it, toward it, at the same time that I disown it. I want to embrace the word women *and* cast it off. I would like to say (to myself and others), Choose if you belong and how. Yet I also see that it is not entirely a matter of choice. Even resisting our inclusion in the category seems inevitably to be possible only in the context of having already internalized containment by it. I don't believe we really have access to some time of innocence *before* we know ourselves as marked by this name nor that we can really reach some *beyond* where the name no longer applies to us.

Yet I would like to find some way of expressing the fluidity of the relation between myself and this category, " 'women," between my "I" and any "we," some way of communicating that the "we" means a more finely nuanced mode of difference than that connoted by the options "same *or* opposite," a more subtle mode of relationship than "self *or* other." When I see myself as a woman speaking among women, I mean to suggest nearness, proximity, affinity, not identity.[5] I long for a way of speaking that honors the fluid impermanence of both my "I" and the group "women." I would like to speak playfully, poetically, *as* a woman, *as* a feminist, knowing that these names can never fully encompass all that I am, that they misname, misidentify, as well as name and identify. Like Diana Fuss I dream of a politics that might "embrace partial, contradictory, permanently unclosed constructions of personal and collective selves and still be faithful, effective."[6] Like Marge Piercy I know that I must relearn to say "I" and "we":

> *She must learn again to speak*
> *starting with I*
> *starting with We*
> *starting as the infant does*
> *with her own true hunger*
> *and pleasure and rage.*[7]

I offer no assumptions about how much of what I have to say may also be true for other women—much less, about what of it might also be relevant to some men. Each of the women whom I imagine within the circle, each of the men whom I imagine at its edge, must discover for themselves what is relevant to them. Feminism, as I understand it, entails not only a recognition of the diversities among us and an attunement to the importance of the subtle as well as the more obvious differences between women, but a *celebration* of that diversity which leads us to view it as enriching rather than as deficit, as enduring rather than as provisional.

This makes evident that it would not simply be premature to essay anything so definitive as *a* psychology of women, but that we must renounce the very project of reducing the plurality of voices to one. What I can bring as my offering can only be notes toward a poetics of the psyche gleaned from my responses to what I have learned from others and from my own history. I speak as a participant in a conversation not as a monologist, what I can contribute is but one of "many kinds of knowing working together or taking turns."[8]

In some ways this serves to make speaking adequately about what it is like to be a woman, speaking in a way that is true to *my* experience and yet also relevant to that of other women, even more troublesome than it seemed a generation or even a decade ago. In other ways it becomes easier. By virtue of not carrying the responsibility of speaking for all, I can speak for myself—in response to others, in the hope of evoking response from others, and in the recognition that I may have other and different things to say later. I am very aware that I am not always clear about all the assumptions that underlie my views (and wonder if any of us are, particularly whether we can ever be fully conscious of our most tacit and deeply held commitments and values), and am grateful for how dialogue with others helps me see contradictions and inadequacies to which I would otherwise remain blind. I know I will continue to speak out of a specific history, as a member of a particular generation and class, raised by my particular parents, taught by my particular teachers, moved by particular books, loved and hurt by particular others.

This should explain why I find Harding's image of virginal in-one-selfness empowering—but also disturbing. For she seems to imagine as ideal a self-sufficiency which I suspect as too like the idealization of autonomy celebrated in those "masculine" psychologies she deplores. My sense of self is a more relational, more contextual one. I see us (us women, and beyond that, us humans) as more intertwined with others, with a community, and more shaped by our particular histories than did she. I am impressed that even Artemis, the Greek goddess most closely resembling Harding's virgin, is rarely found alone but rather almost always in the company of her nymphs. I remember that the maenads, women who have cast off their socially defined roles as wives and mothers, get in touch with their most instinctual selves in the context of a *thiasos*, a ritual community. I have learned that this is so for me as well: I discover myself in the context of my engagements with others —though in that context I also discover my differences from others.

Foremothers and Forefathers

Because there are few explicit rituals of female initiation among us today, it is not always clear how we learned to think about ourselves in the particular way that we do, or from whom. But as I reflect on my own process I am aware of how varied my initiators have been. Many have been women: my mother, my sister, my daughter, the spinster school-teachers of my youth, my peer friends all along the way, my lovers. Also the feminist theorists, past and present, whom I have come to regard as colleagues, and, perhaps even more importantly, the women poets and novelists whom I read and reread. I have also learned much from ancient mythology and from my own dreams. I have learned from times of joy and from experiences of failure and loss, isolation and suffering. And from my body.

To think freshly about myself requires that I listen carefully to all these teachers. But I sometimes find it painfully difficult to be true to my feminist commitments and my deep bonds with women—and also to myself, all the twists and turns of my own history. For though so many of my initiators have been women, many have also been men. I am profoundly aware that I enter the ritual space not only as a mother's daughter but also as a father's daughter. Nonetheless, it is also clear to me that the judgment of the women within the circle matters more than that of the men at its periphery.

I live with a woman I love and am proud to call myself a lesbian. I write mostly about women's lives and experiences. I write in a way that I feel may be to some degree at least a woman's way, a way which interweaves the intellectual and the personal, the conceptual and the poetic—not because I have consciously looked for a female form but because that's how I have found I can most truly express what I have to say. Most of those with whom I share my work in progress, who become part of the process, are women. When I read contemporary literature, it is women's writing that moves me most deeply—Jane Rule, Isabel Allende, Christa Wolf, Alice Walker, Toni Morrison.

BUT.

Just that. But . . .

These women feel like sisters. I feel blessed to be among them, but they are not mothers, not mentors, and there are times when I sorely feel the absence of motherly mentors.

Yet I am also haunted by a motherly voice which says:

You are not committed enough to women
You are not a real feminist
You are not a real lesbian

I don't really know whose voice that is.

No one has ever said that directly to me.

But I hear the voice speaking.

It's not my mother's voice (though, of course, not entirely unrelated to her voice) but somehow The Mother's.

Her words seem more cruel, more punitive, more judgmental than the words of The Father, the male superego, whom I've also heard talking to me all my life—but almost always in a way that felt challenging, encouraging, approving.

It's as though The Mother wants me all to herself—as though she were even more possessive than I've experienced The Father as being—and also that she wants me to be just *like* her, the ideal, the perfect, the completely woman-identified woman.

I understand this (intellectually) on the basis of feminist rereadings of Freud (like those of Chodorov, Dinnerstein, and even Downing!) which point out the primal, primary experiences that pull both mothers and daughters toward fusion longing (and fear). I find especially relevant a passage from Dinnerstein's *The Mermaid and the Minotaur* which expresses her sense that the move from "matriarchy" to "patriarchy" was something positively important for women's psychology not just something imposed by men. Dinnerstein understands this transition (whether or not it ever happened historically) to represent the "surmounting" of our "deep yearning for magic superhuman protection which is a carry-over from infancy" and the acceptance that "the limited, puny human power, the power that we ourselves actually embody, is the only kind of power on which we can realistically rely." She sees fathers playing an essential role in moving daughters to self-responsibility out of passive symbiosis. Although Dinnerstein sees clearly how the reliance on human will and reason she associates with patriarchy has gone too far, how desperately we now need to create something different, she is persuaded that what is now required is *not* a return to "matriarchy," to *that* sense of women's culture.[9]

Indeed, it sometimes occurs to me that perhaps fathers by stepping between mothers and daughters may help females move from daughterhood to sisterhood, from fusion toward a more mutual, reciprocal woman-woman relationship. Obviously this doesn't always happen; fathers may play much less beneficent roles; women may move beyond fusion along other paths. Bit it may happen.

In my book on same-sex love I wrote about two "women's cultures," the Amazons and the maenads. It interested me to discover that neither were "matriarchies." The Amazons were a sisterhood of daughters who had so freed themselves of the mother that her name was in dispute or forgotten. What they acknowledged was that they were daughters of Ares. They worshiped Artemis, not as a Mother but as the Sister Goddess. Rulership among them was shared among three sisters. The maenads *were* mothers; unmarried girls, virgins, were excluded from their rites. But they were mothers who had (temporarily, for the liminal period of the ritual) abandoned their "motherhood," their husbands and children, their domestic roles and responsibilities, in order to gather together to celebrate their own instinctual, sexual, creative female being. Except for Dionysos males were forbidden access to their mysteries. But somehow the presence of the god who is both preeminently phallic *and* without his phallus, the "womanly" god who allows himself to be penetrated, allowed the women access to the fullness of their own female energy. It seems to me too simple to dismiss these traditions as stories men tell about women. I hear something true in them.

Perhaps we need fathers' daughters and mothers' daughters. Yes, we should all be both. Yes, we *are* all both—but not in neat, tidy, identical, or guilt-free, confusion-free ways. I am acutely aware of the degree to which I am a father's daughter and of how important it is not to hide that, for to do so would mean being present in the circle dishonestly.

I see this to be true at the personal level. My mother's aging—she is almost ninety, going blind—is so difficult for her, for everyone. She is so filled with rage at all the ways she did not get to use her gifts, to live her "real life" because of having always been a good daughter, a good wife, a good daughter-in-law, a good mother. She is so bitter about what never happened and what never will—and so self-absorbed. I ache for her. I know the truth of her complaints. I know how much of what happened in her life and what didn't has to do with history, with structure, with "patriarchy," with my father. I know—and agree with —the "feminist" critique of her situation. I understand the ways in which her rage is an almost too long delayed *affirmation* of her own desires and her own perspective. But I sense the "pity" in my empathy. And I hear the voice inside me which protests so strenuously: I don't want to grow old like her.

What this means to me I articulate more fully in chapter 5 where I explore my ambivalent response to the figure of the Crone. Here it is enough to say: I love this woman. I felt especially close to her in preadolescence and then again in the early years of my marriage when my children were small, and once more in my forties and early fifties when I was entranced by my new discovery of "women's culture," absorbed by my engagements with women students, colleagues, friends, lovers, women writers, womanly deities. She was in her late sixties and seventies then, writing woman-centered poetry, getting published, surrounded by women friends. We were living in the same world.

In adolescence I felt closer to my father who blessed my intellectual ambitions—as I did again when I began graduate school and when I began teaching, and as I do now. Though he is today in many ways a *new* father, different from the one I remember from earlier years, what draws me close to him now is his new-found gentleness and patience, his awkward attempts to give my mother the everyday tokens of physical affection for which she hungers but which were never before part of his repertoire. I cherish his new willingness to be dependent and vulnerable with me. I am grateful for the modestly tentative and tender ways he shares his garnered wisdom with my children and grandchildren.

The voice inside says: I want to grow old like *him*.

And I may. For I am like him in many ways. Indeed, the woman I live with often tells me, "I never imagined that in choosing a woman as my life-partner, I'd be choosing my daddy but that seems to be what I've done." Sometimes that's meant as an affirmation, sometimes it's said in anger or regret. Most times we both feel it's true. Her daddy, my daddy. There's not much difference.

But when I speak of being a father's daughter, I am not primarily speaking personally, but also (and perhaps more significantly) intellectually. Lou Salome, who met Freud when she was in her fifties, he in his sixties (at a time when she was more widely recognized as an important cultural figure than he), and became his most intimate friend during the last decades of his life, once wrote to him: your's is "the father-face which has presided over my life."[10] I think that there is a sense in which that is true for me as well. I keep returning to Freud, keep rereading, keep learning more, keep having everything turned upside down, keep being grateful for his wisdom and courage and his care for us suffering human beings. There are other "forefathers" from whom I keep learning, especially the Greek tragedians, but also Nietzsche and Jung and Rilke and Thomas Mann. I have learned from these patriarchs about myself, about women (and men, too, of course)—though often by fighting, arguing, reframing.

We have all learned that we do not get to choose our parents. My sense is that we do not fully get to choose our teachers either, and that sometimes we may experience a painful tension between whom we've really been taught by and those whom our political commitments would lead us to want to name. "A painter," I recently read, "is drawn to his ancestry by a homing instinct that works below 'strategy.' In this he is both free and not free. This is not like shopping around for a style to adopt. It is deeper and more compulsive. It is to know one's heritage, its limits, the challenges these present. Each bloodline entails responsibilities." When the author distinguishes "the organic complexities of a serious artist's relation to the past" from "a shallow puppet show (*of*) hostility to one's ancestors," I understand him to be saying more clearly than I have been able to why for me participation in the ritual requires honoring both the mothers and the fathers.[11]

The *core* issue still seems to me to be our own relation to our female sources and our feminine souls—to mother, sister, self. BUT part of fully doing *that* seems to involve also honoring father, brother, son. I imagine a "women's culture" that includes men—but not on the old terms. Dionysos not Zeus.

For now I want simply to reaffirm my conviction that precisely as a feminist I know I need to honor the fathers. I know that I am untrue to myself if I disavow the truth of my own history in order to please the other women in the ritual circle. I have come to believe that part of how the myth of difference wounds us lies in how easily it seduces us to yield to the pull toward separatism. The insistence on difference so readily leads us into reifying the announced differences as unbridgeable or as inevitably generating antagonism.

Rites of Separation

I find myself filled with sadness when I contemplate the anger, the pain, and the isolation that gender consciousness and gender confusion seem so often to engender, and perturbed by the degree of fear and suspicion of otherness that any consideration of gender seems to inspire. We seem so often to meet members of the other gender or members of our own who are living their response to the wounds of genderedness differently from ourselves with distrust and apprehension.

Women and men often feel radically estranged from one another, as do homosexuals and heterosexuals. We are so drawn to withdraw into small homogeneous groups that sometimes among groups of feminists or lesbians (the groups I know best) it seems as though there is *no* other whose experience or ideology is sufficiently akin to our own to bring us the confirmation, the identity, for which we long. How I wish we might instead be able to turn with compassion to the others who are responding in diverse ways to the same wounds that inflict us. How healing it would be were we able to recognize that we are each living out our particular response not only for ourselves but also for one another.

I see us as all coparticipants in a time of transitional consciousness about the meaning of gender. It isn't in place as it seemed to be when I was growing up. My own conviction is that none of us quite know anymore what being male or being female means nor how the feminine and the masculine or women and men (or even women and women or men and men) can most creatively relate. The confusion touches all of us—no matter how confidently we may try to live within the old definitions or to proclaim our adherence to an alternative vision.

Of course there was never a promise that the raising of consciousness (about gender—or any other facet of our existence) would issue in increased harmony or happiness. Indeed, Kierkegaard, Nietzsche, and Freud all warned us of the contrary consequence. Even Sophocles taught that Oedipus's illumination leads, at least immediately, only to his self-blinding: he has been shown more than he can bear to see. As epigraph to my book on the Greek goddesses I used a quote from James Hillman to the effect that myths don't tell us how, they only help us to question, imagine, go deeper. I believe the same is true of all genuine consciousness-raising: it doesn't address just ego-consciousness, doesn't speak only to our longing for rational theory and explanation or for pragmatic solutions, but helps us to enter the complexity of our situations more deeply, with more love of the perplexities themselves and of those caught up in them. Freud speaks of therapy as accomplishing at best the transition from neurotic misery to common unhappiness. Perhaps that is precisely what *therapeia,* attention to soul, can yield: it can help move us from disabling anger and hurt to compassionate acceptance of our common unhappiness—"common" meaning not only "ordinary" but "shared."

My years of involvement with Greek goddess traditions and their illumination of female experience have helped me to appreciate the multidimensionality of the female point of view. I know full well that there is more than one female perspective on gender issues; indeed, that I myself see differently at different times. So in trying to clarify my own approach, it seems natural to ask, Through what goddess am I looking?

I have discovered that each of the goddesses represents a way of being in the world, a way of ordering experience, a mode of perception, and so see each as offering a distinct way of understanding gender. I want to know which goddess presides in *this* context where I want to join in a celebration of women's mysteries which welcomes men as onlookers though not as active participants.

It is evident to me that it is not primarily Demeter, a goddess who validates only the mother-daughter bond, who represents the celebration of fusion and the denial of separateness. Because in Demeter's world all wounds are male-created, she seeks to create a world from which men would be excluded. (Though there is a sense in which Demeter is present as that motherly voice before which I willy-nilly feel I have to justify myself.)

Nor is it primarily Hera. For Hera represents a commitment to the ideal of heterosexual complementarity—and the rage and envy that appear when oppression is discovered where one expected equality. (Though I accept Hera's implicit claim that separatism is only a temporary solution, that we need somehow to come to terms with men, to at least acknowledge that they are *there*.)

Nor is the view I am putting forward here compatible with Artemis's celebration of the feminine as a natural biological reality, not dependent on social context or definition. (Although in chapter 4, where I try to articulate a poetics of the female body, Artemis will be duly recognized.)

Athene's perspective, too, is different from the one I'm focusing on here, for she represents a disparagement of the conventionally feminine and calls women to identify instead with those capacities and attributes traditionally reserved to the male. (Yet I value Athene's emphasis on seeing everything in terms of its relevance to communal life and imagine her assenting to a socially constructed view of gender.)

No, my viewing here is clearly primarily shaped by Aphrodite who blesses relationships between man and man or woman with woman as wholeheartedly as those between woman and man and reminds us that there is always pain and loss in all our experiences of passion and intimacy. Aphrodite encourages me to honor both the blessings and wounds of gendered existence. In a later chapter I speak more directly of my gratitude for the joy-bringing experiences intimately associated with my female embodiment. Here I need first to look at what I call the shadow face of gender.

We have come to recognize gender, the human experience of sexual difference, the *consciousness* of being female or male, as not simply a biological given but as a psychosocial construct. As Freud understood, one is not born but made a woman; it is just as true that one is not born but made a man.

Freud believed that the discovery of gender is correlative with human consciousness, with the discovery of self and other. Initially he understood this to happen vis-à-vis sibling experience. Both boys and girls, he said, discover their gender identity by discovering how their bodies differ from the other's and both focus on the most visible emblem, the penis. He saw the discovery as traumatic for both, evoking envy in the girl and castration fear in the boy. Later, when Freud became more aware of the importance of the pre-Oedipal period, he discussed the beginnings of gender awareness in terms of the infant's relation to the mother. Having or not having birth-giving capacity, a less visible sign, becomes the mark of differentiation. Others, extrapolating from Freud, have suggested that perhaps we first become aware of gender when we encounter the prohibition of desire directed toward a same-sex parent and for the first time discover that gender matters, that it determines whom we may or may not love.[12] We might note that whichever story we choose to believe, gender is related to a not-having, a loss, a wound.

I'm not sure that there is one invariant story. I don't even claim to know which is *my* story—though I have many vivid memories from the era in my life before my brother was born when I was two, and think I already knew then that in some ways I was more like my mother than my father. I'm not sure, though, that these necessarily seemed the most important ways.

No matter which theory we prefer, I'm persuaded that learning what it means to be female rather than male is a process, not a one-moment event. Nonetheless, the complex cultural meanings added on to the "facts" of biological difference are imposed so subtly and so early that we don't ever have a sense of what "woman" or "man" mean apart from their socialized definitions. For not only are individual men and women "made," but so also are the categories "man" and "woman."

It has become relatively easy for us to admit to the distortions inherent in the two-gender system. We see how it may make us more different than we really are, how it ignores that there are more differences on any parameter within each gender than there are between average representatives of each gender. We also see how much has been smuggled into the male/female polarity that doesn't quite fit. As Freud already acknowledged, gender identity is not always necessarily congruent with anatomical sex and neither automatically determines object choice. By now many of us recognize the falsity of the presumed causal and inevitable relationship between anatomical sex, social gender, and sexual desire.

The gender system exaggerates differences and fails to create stable categories. It fails to account for diversity, for the subversive complexity of actual lives. It seems impossible to make a two-column list of attributes that stays in place, that yields a coherent, stable meaning for masculine or feminine. We see how the fantasy of opposites distorts, how viewing activity/passivity (which Freud said were the only possible *psychological* meanings of masculine/feminine) as opposites leads us to exaggerate each—so that activity becomes aggression or even more vividly, sadism, and passivity, masochism. The two-column model suggests that being assertive and being rational necessarily go together, that being self-confident and being vulnerable are necessarily incompatible. At the most, the system would allow that we might be one consciously, the other unconsciously.

Thus many of us have learned to reject these equations, these antitheses, even to wonder how anyone could ever have accepted them. Yet I suspect that despite their incoherence and their oppressiveness, these traditional images of male and female continue to have more power over most of us than we fully realize. They live on in our unconscious and, particularly in times of stress, may shape our feelings and even our actions in ways that take us by surprise.

When we first understand the gender/sex distinction, we are likely to think of gender as referring to attributes added on to biological differences. We are used to thinking of "man" and "woman" as nouns and the gender attributes as adjectives qualifying these abiding substances.[13] So much conspires to encourage us to believe that there is a mimetic or causal relation between gender and sex, between being a woman and having a female anatomy.[14]

It may be dizzying to discover that that is too simple, that it may, indeed, be the other way around! I put the quotation marks around "facts" a page or so ago to suggest how our way of seeing our bodies, of picturing our biology, is itself a social construction. We view our bodies in a particular way because of how we view gender. It is difficult at first to acknowledge how strange and arbitrary and fetishistic it is to regard an external body part, the penis, as *the* mark of personal identity.

Having learned to distinguish sex and gender, it seems that we now need to unlearn the distinction. "Deconstruction" has destabilized not only our understanding of gender but the very disparity between sex and gender, the natural and the social. In an odd way, we see as "natural" what we've learned to see as such. Gender is a social category, but so also, it turns out, is sex. We have no access to a prelinguistic, presocial biological facticity, to an innocent experience of our bodies "before" we learned to name them. Once we see that the very emphasis on anatomical difference is itself an interpretation, it becomes even more obvious how much else has been sneaked in as indispensable corollary.

The traditional, socially validated images present themselves as "natural," essential, archetypal. Yet these images, which lie deep in all of us almost irrespective of whether or not we consciously subscribe to them, are constructed from a predominantly male perspective and so represent mostly men's experience of self and other. In the next chapter I will explore why these male images have tended to be based on a "fantasy of opposites" and how women might help exorcise their power.

But here, too, our consideration of the social construction of gender must include acknowledgment of the *politics* of that construction, the motives that underlie it, the oppression that results from it. For the two-gender system not only emphasizes difference but also imposes a hierarchical interpretation of difference. We need to become more conscious of the power politics inherent in our naming, to see more clearly how dividing up humans on the basis of gender is in the service of the reproduction of patriarchy and heterosexism. Because culture and language encourage males to see their perspective as the human perspective, a psychology of gender has always been primarily a psychology of women. Because males are regarded as universal persons, only females are viewed as gendered![15] The imposition of the traditional gender system functions as a rite of separation, it separates men from women and women from the fully human—as Muriel Rukeyser playfully points out in her poem "Myth" in which the old and blind Oedipus again meets up with the Sphinx:

"When I asked, What walks on four legs in the morning,
two at noon, and three in the evening, you answered,
Man.   You didn't say anything about woman."
"When you say Man," said Oedipus, "you include women
too. Everybody knows that."   She said,
"That's what you think."[16]

As women have tried to name how the old definitions don't fit their inner experience but delimit their outer possibilities, some have asserted that there are no real differences, psychologically speaking, between women and men except those imposed by society. Others have insisted that there are enormous differences—but not the ones ascribed by male theorists. Femaleness, these women say, is in its essence an unwounded and unwounding reality. On this view all the wounding suffered by women has been inflicted on them by The Father, by patriarchy. What wounds is having been "torn from a woman, from women, from ourselves,"[17] too soon, too radically. In an all female world we would all be whole.

To my mind, another fairy tale. This demonization of males, of heterosexuality, and heterosexism represents an enormous effort to deny the shadow side of our own lives. We project all the pain and ugliness of human life onto males, evade our own finitude, ignore that for us, too, separation from the mother is a necessary and painful reality—though it is indeed different to separate from another like ourselves than from one who is not. I believe it to be dangerously evasive to repress the reality of gender (and thus render it unconscious) or the reality of the wounds of gendered existence.

The old definitions of gender were oppressive to both women and men. The old definitions and institutions not only cut females off from such "masculine" attributes as self-assertiveness and rationality and from access to outward forms of power, but also cut males off from their feelings and from the enjoyment of intimacy. But because the oppression was not isomorphic it did not become part of our culture's *conscious* awareness until women began to speak for themselves.

What may be most unsettling about feminism is women's resolution that we are no longer willing to be "the Other," the object, the defined, no longer willing to accept male experience as the paradigm of human experience. We are not castrated males; it does not follow that because men have an Oedipus complex women have an Electra complex, nor that women have an animus because men have an anima.

As women have begun to claim the right to define themselves, they have said: the given descriptions don't do justice to our experience. In naming this, they have made us all aware of the degree to which the dominant assumptions about gender are patriarchal, that is, shaped by a culture in which men dominate. As such, they are assumptions oppressive to women—and, also, we are beginning to see, to males. Thus we now all see and feel wounds which were earlier invisible. Being female feels like a wound or curse rather than a blessing—but so does being male. The wounds are different; there are gender-specific pathologies, but we seem to be at a time when at least some members of each gender are experiencing gender as wound. Each feels itself to be inferior.

The patriarchal interpretation of gender made us so different from one another and so channeled gender interactions into dominance-submission patterned relationships, that eventually the isolation, suspicion, and imbalance, the *unreality,* became intolerable. But the erasure of the agreed-upon system in which males were the namers and the norm is itself also anxiety-creating—and this anxiety seems to engender further hostility and isolation, suspicion and separation.

The substantive grammar, accepting "man/woman" as nouns, imposes an artificial binary division between the sexes and an artificial internal coherence. The apparent naturalness of the binary system hides from us that one gender has coherent meaning only in relation to the other gender, that the two-gender system implies heterosexuality. Recognition of this has led Monique Wittig and others to refuse to participate in this pronominal system which requires that all of us be "shes" or "hes." They believe we need to disown the very category of "women" because it defines us as "not-men."[18]

The fantasy of discarding or transcending the categories has enormous appeal. We may feel elation as we imagine ourselves free of them. But just as we can't really get to a "before," I doubt that we can get to an "after." I have to confess, also, that to my mind there is something false about deconstructionism. It seems to be yet another mind game.

I enjoy the mental exercise of seeing through the categories of sex and gender, but I am aware how easily that leads to a falsely utopian sense of having overcome their dominion.

I am not the first woman to note that this dismantling of agency and authorship arises just as women are claiming the subject-position, that this discounting of all voices arises just as the existence of "other" voices becomes undeniable. There is something strangely a-social in this emphasis on the social construction of all categories, something which serves to hide the role of power and oppression in these constructions. It is all well and good to recognize the arbitrariness of the social construction of gender, but we still have to take seriously that these things *are* constructed, they do shape our lives and our consciousness.

I am wary of our getting too tricky. I see how the longing for identity and community is not only male, not only oppressive, but also a human need. It is too simple to blame it all on patriarchy. I see how the wish for a coherent self and for group affiliation comes with being human. I believe it is imperative for us to recognize this, for the recognition makes forgiveness possible—and also the creation of alternative perspectives which might *amplify* (in the rich Jungian sense) without necessarily replacing the long-established images. The importance of forgiveness was brought home to me by Isabel Allende's novel *The House of the Spirits,* which ends with a reconciliation (based on remembrance not denial) between a granddaughter and the abusive family patriarch. There is nothing sentimental about this ending, though at first it seems shocking, impossible—but then one sees: only on this basis can there be a future.

A Poetics of Gender

I find myself more interested in the *poetics* than the *politics* of gender, in exploring the ways we humans imagine sexual difference and what longings and fears these various images betray. The hope, as I see it, is to get past our literalism around gender, to admit that "man" and "woman" are fictive terms, images, which hide *and* reveal. To accept gender as *made*, as a *poesis*, means seeing it as always still in the process of being made and remade. I like Judith Butler's proposal that we come to look upon "gender as a complexity whose totality is permanently deferred." Gender in this perspective is a "performative" rather than an ontological category. "Woman is an ongoing discursive practice, open to intervention and resignification; gender is a set of repeated acts which may congeal, rigidify, and then loosen again."[19] As poets of gender, we can engage in the exploration of alternative perspectives and perhaps even in the creation of new ones.

Actually, there has never really been but one myth of gender, but rather always a rich variety of myths which may seem to contradict one another but to which we may nonetheless find we can give simultaneous credence.

There is, for example, perhaps even more seductive than the myth of difference, *the myth of transcendence*, of nongenderedness. I have dismissed this myth of a return to a prelinguistic, pregendered existence as an impossible dream, since wholeness can always be known only retrospectively as a fantasied "before." And yet, and yet . . . There is truth as well in these fantasies of simple wholeness in a single-gendered world. Such fantasies are prominent in many myths, particularly myths about how it was in the beginning: Gaia is a mother goddess who creates parthenogenetically; Atum a god who creates through masturbatory ejaculation. The fantasies and the myths may both have their origin in our earliest experience, and may bear testimony to valid, creative hopes.

For, if gender is psychosocial, if it is consciousness of being female or male, then early infancy (like Eden) is in this sense pregender. (Adam and Eve were male and female in Eden but not yet aware of it nor of the pain associated with gender identity. When they are expelled from the garden, they learn that henceforward there will be enmity between man and woman. Adam learns that being male means toil and sweat, Eve that being female means pain and dependency.) Psychologically, sexual differences don't exist until they are consciously experienced. Freud articulated this by referring to early childhood as a time when we are bisexual or, perhaps more accurately, polysexual, polymorphously "perverse" (i.e., perverse by the terms of the dominant gender system). He also recognized that if a nongender-differentiated reality is there initially, then in a sense it is *always* there, albeit unconsciously. For nothing in the unconscious ever dies. The memory persists, stirring nostalgia and hope.

Indeed, it may be because of that memory that most of us at least some of the time experience our own genderedness, being female *or* male, as the discovery of a wound, a lost wholeness. Perhaps we need this myth *as* a myth to sustain our hopes of a less wounded, less wounding, being here.

The myth of transcendence, of the irrelevance of gender, easily transmutes into a separatist fantasy, *the myth of sameness:* the pretence that there is only one gender, or that all the truly valuable human attributes are to be found only among members of that gender, or that only with members of one's own sex can one have true intimacy.

Today many women and men are turning to same-sex bonding for the confirmation they might earlier have hoped to receive from relationships with members of the other sex. This includes not only those choosing explicitly homosexual life-styles, but also those who consciously turn to others of their own gender for their primary experiences of intimacy and emotional support. (As most people in most cultures may always have done—for it may be only the "invention" of romantic love and its cultural validation as the primary basis of the marital bond that created among us the expectation that the closest other would be a member of the other gender.)

Since men were (at least on the surface) the victors in the traditional gender system and since it was created at least in part as a way of transcending their sense of woundedness and inferiority, it is not too surprising that the criticism of heterosexual bonds should first have been voiced by women. But now many men I know, including many heterosexual men, are acknowledging the importance in their lives of deep, psychologically complex, emotionally vulnerable relationships to other men. I think not only of such publicly visible men as James Hillman and Robert Bly but of many others, less prominent and often less articulate. These men seek to affirm the nurturing that men can give one another and to describe how it differs from mother love. They speak of how important it is to free the father-son relationship from being understood only in the context of the primacy of the mother-son bond, a context which inevitably casts the father as rival and castrator.

For both women and men the turn to same-sex relationship reflects a conviction that we become who we are not so much by contrast as by analogy, through an intensification of our own way of being, and through mirroring. Confirmation comes from another whose experience is close to one's own and with whom one can participate in a shared exploration. The assumption is that really only like can know like, that only like can heal like, that one can learn what it is to be a woman not primarily from experience with men but from oneself and from interaction with other women.

Yet the myth of sameness *is* a myth. We discover when we turn to others of the same sex as ourselves that they are not after all just like us, but rather bewilderingly, confusingly, challengingly different. Paradoxical as it might seem, many of us find that there may be more possibility of a real acceptance of heterogeneity, separateness, otherness within a same-sex relationship than in a heterosexual one. For here the otherness is somehow within bounds, not so extreme as to preclude any real intercourse.

Another response to the recognition that being male or female is to feel incomplete has been to look to the other gender for completion, for healing and wholeness. We might call this the *myth of complementarity*. Luce Iragaray calls it "the old dream of symmetry."[20] Adherence to this myth grows out of a conviction that we learn who we are primarily by contrast, by discovering our difference from another. (It may well be that this understanding of identity may be less natural to females than to males who come to self-consciousness with the discovery of being not just separate from the mother but different from her.)

I see how there is something about primary relationships that seems to encourage the notion that where one partner is weak, the other will be strong; that together we will be as one whole person. As I have discovered how in my present involvement with a female mate, I often find myself being toward her much as my husband in my heterosexual marriage had been toward me— stable and reliable but emotionally reserved, patient and understanding but somewhat patronizing—I've seen how much what we ordinarily think of as gender roles may be just relationship roles. (Though, because of gender stereotyping and the expectations it creates, there may be even less room to create a pattern of complementation that really derives from the gifts and needs of the two individuals in heterosexual relationships than in same-sex ones.) Nonetheless, there seems to be something inherently unstable about relationships based on complementarity; eventually one or the other partner will tire of the deformation that trying to conform to the other entails.

Because we are wounded creatures, we tend to fear being further wounded, to fear otherness, to fear dependency, and to misconstrue interdependence as domination. Because the differences between another and myself may seem to be so great as to be well-nigh intolerable, in seeking to establish a relationship I may try to make that other more like myself. Because we can't tolerate the heterogeneity, we may seek to dominate or destroy the otherness of the other. Thus heterosexual encounters often come to be contaminated by patterns of dominance and submission—even when we may all want something quite different. (And, of course, this can happen in lesbian and gay relationships as well.)

Thus the myth of complementation easily slips into the myth we focused on before, *the myth of hierarchical difference,* which sees the other sex as the "opposite"sex (and usually as the "inferior" or "superior" sex). Thinking in terms of polarities and hierarchies may to some degree come more naturally to males (as we'll discuss in the next chapter), but it is a way of thinking common to all of us. Yet we know that there are polytheistic cultures less caught in dualistic thinking than ours. My interest in Greek and Egyptian mythology in part grows out of my hope that these polytheisms can help us see ways in which we might get free of the thrall of same/opposite thinking, might come to accept our predilection for antithetical thinking and yet not be tyrannized by it.

The *myth of diversity* acknowledges the differences between men and women without hierarchical evaluation and actually accords more attention to the differences within genders. It celebrates plurality, variety, polyphony. But the recognition of diversity also means accepting wounds, limitation, finitude. The two become many who need and support one another, fail and betray one another, are like and unlike, intimate and distant—and unmistakably, inextricably interconnected. (This myth is often upheld in tandem with the *myth of a human continuum,* which maintains that what we all share as humans is what is more important than what might distinguish women from men.)

The myth of diversity has radical implications not only for our understanding of gender but for our conception of personhood. If we move beyond traditional images of gender difference, we may also move toward a different image of personal identity, one which puts much less emphasis on autonomy, coherence, stability, completion. The myth implies a more polytheistic, always provisional sense of self (albeit one already implicit in Freud's vision of the fluid shape-shifting relation within the psyche between the ego and the unconscious).

The myth of diversity, of destabilized groups and selves, has enormous appeal, but it is also scary and chaotic, and in a sense perhaps too abstract. It ignores the degree to which we all inevitably live within the two-gender myth and can't entirely leap beyond it. It recognizes the resistance to identity at the heart of psychic life, and how illusory is the ego's claim of mastery, but it may fail to see that it is precisely the ego's role to keep showing up and making that claim. We seem to need these always vulnerable, always tentative assumptions of identity—and their disruption. Thus we may learn that identity is always fictitious, that it, too, involves a *poetics*.

None of these myths are entirely satisfactory. Perhaps we need them all; perhaps even as individuals we actually recognize the relevance to our own experience of several of them. Perhaps acknowledging each *as* a myth helps us move beyond taking any as literally true, helps us see why only a poetic language, a language of image, can do justice to the complexity of our experience.

We live in a strange in-between time. I think of Nietzsche's Madman announcing what seems to him a clearly established fact—that God is dead—and then discovering that, although the death *has* occurred, most people don't know it yet. Similarly, I believe that we live in a time when the two-gender system undergirded by patriarchy is dead, but (because its death is still more an inward realization than an outward reality) most of us don't know it yet. The oppression of patriarchal culture, of The Father, still clearly persists in our economic, social, and political institutions, in language, in patterns of family life, in female self-denigration and in male assumptions of superiority. Yet at the same time there exists an inner recognition—sometimes noticeable only as a slight twinge of dis-ease—that patriarchy is dead, that its ideology can no longer be taken for granted as authoritative, that it no longer works in us with unquestioned albeit unconscious fiat. It is no longer obvious that masculinity is superior, that men are better off—or even just what masculinity (or femininity) really is.

Yes, men still have social privilege, but they no longer feel sure of having it nor sure of their right to have it. The ground is moving beneath them. Naturally, the response is defense and attack, and pleas for help. Many men are becoming aware of what their reliance on rationality, power, and dominance has done to them. Critiques of the "male mystique," of the myths of male superiority, comparable to the early feminist literature of twenty years ago, are beginning to appear not only among the poets but on the drugstore racks.

But the new insecurity among men has also inevitably *heightened* the misogyny of some. Some men believe that the balance of power has really already shifted to women, that women no longer seem to need men for their own fulfillment (though they may use them to have children). Such men often say they envy women the communal support they receive from one another. I believe they are at least to some degree re-experiencing the envy of women and the fear of being different from them that led to the assertion of male supremacy in the first place. They sense again the real fragility inherent in maleness and the mysterious otherness of females. It is now again evident that being male and being human are not equivalent, that being male is but one form, one aspect, of being human. If the longing is to be whole in oneself, complete, and if being gendered means being limited, finite, then gender is wound.

Whether we are homosexual or heterosexual, whether we are women or men, the real issue, I believe, is the acceptance of our own particularity and finitude and of the reality of otherness. The hope lies in our coming to see that we all (men and women, lesbian, gay, and straight) feel wounded, feel inferior, and in our coming to experience this inferiority as a way of being brought in touch with the *inferiores*, with the creative, transformative depths of experience.[21] Our sense of our own vulnerability, our openness to change, might then bring compassion toward the others whom we know to be as wounded as ourselves, rather than the rage, the exploitation, the withdrawal that seem so often to be all we are capable of at present.

We cannot know at this time what gender *will* mean. We cannot know how necessary it *will* be to think in terms of gender. We can certainly see the virtue of being free of thinking always primarily along this fault line, in terms of this vector of difference—and yet also see that fantasies of nongenderedness are fantasies which deny otherness, separation, finitude, and particularity. They express our longing to be everything, to have everything, to be or become without wound.

We try to forget that none of the ways we choose to live our gendered lives are fully satisfying, that we cannot after all have or be everything. Truly to accept this is also to recognize that others who choose different paths from our own do so on our behalf. They live for us, as well as for themselves. Can we come to celebrate this variety rather than to bemoan it? I am not at all sure that there is any peculiarly female wisdom, yet I sense that it does often seem easier for women to learn that experiences of woundedness, of fragmentation and vulnerability, are as real, as ultimate, as experiences of wholeness. How truly I hope that we might all come to accept that, and what accepting it asks of us. How truly I look forward to that ritual occasion when all of us will join together to honor the wounds and gifts of each.

·3·

RITES OF EXORCISM

As I hope the last chapter of this book makes manifest, I am deeply persuaded that it is time to move beyond a focus on the psychology of women to a psychology of the human, indeed beyond psychology to a logos, a poetics, that includes all those forms of life that live on earth with us. But I also believe we needed first to recover, reclaim, redeem, renew, reanimate, reinterpret, recompose, recycle, remember, and repossess the psychology of women. All these words for doing it anew suggest that to go forward we first needed to go back. Only thus have we become strong and clear enough to move outside our sequestered circle, aware of having learned some things we need to say to everyone.

We women have for so long been objects not subjects, the defined not the definers, the "other" in Simone de Beauvoir's phrase, that it is hard not to be strident as we claim the privilege of speaking for ourselves. It is hard not to be angry, to forget that male attempts to name how they see women are often undertaken out of care and respect, and with an honest acknowledgment of the difficulties and limitations inherent in such projects. It is equally hard not to be conciliatory, to agree from the outset that the differences between women and men are superficial and that *really* we are all alike, or that these differences are complementary and thus easily reconcilable.

I am persuaded that the notion that the only alternatives are identity or polarity is singularly inappropriate to a woman's attempt to say what women are like. I am also persuaded that to speak relevantly about a fresh visioning of the psychology of women requires first a reviewing of the history of how depth psychology has viewed women.

Somehow we need to find a way of exorcising these old images, of ridding ourselves of their oppressive influence. To do that ritually entails summoning these voices forth not ignoring or repressing them; it means dispossessing them of power or perhaps transforming that power into a more beneficent energy as, according to Aeschylus, the fearful Erinyes were transformed into the gentle Eumenides. Exorcisms are purification rituals. As Mary Daly says, naming the demons that block our passage makes possible a fresh naming, a truth telling, an original summoning of words.[1]

I imagine a ritual. "We," a group of women, are assembled in the forest clearing. It is night. We are chanting the names of our ancestors. We call out the names of our foremothers and our forefathers. We thank each for what they have given us; we remind each of how they have betrayed us. Each woman's litany is her own. Some names reappear often, some only once. Those whom I remember, others may forget. Where I praise, another may curse. We begin with our mothers. "I am Christine, daughter of Herta, daughter of Johanna, daughter of a German peasant whose name I have never heard spoken, daughter also of H.D., of Lou Salome, of Sappho." We had meant to praise but we find ourselves also cursing them for leaving us "wildly unmothered." We begin then to name the fathers, to express our anger at them for tearing us from our mothers, from ourselves, from Her. Anger, violence mount. We are surprised by all the ugly words, the murderous rage, that come spewing forth. But we are not afraid. The ritual must be completed. We speak these words here so that we need not speak them outside the ritual space. When we have named all the names, uttered all the curses, we fall down exhausted. At dawn we arise refreshed. We embrace one another. As we leave the sacred circle we can be heard humming a tune —wordless as yet.

The point of the ritual is not so much exorcising the male voices, as exorcising our anger at those voices and our own possession by the habits of thought, the antithetical and normative thinking that we associate, for partly valid reasons, with a male perspective. For "unless we acknowledge and confront these histories and claim them as our own, we will remain victims rather than heirs."[2] As I have already affirmed, I believe very strongly in the virtue of honoring our ancestors, our forefathers as well as our foremothers, of recognizing them as there to be learned from and not simply to be overcome, and of acknowledging the inescapable presence and influence of both the long ago matristic past and of the recorded voices of the more recent past. The homage to the concrete, the embodied, the historical dimensions of human life that feminism has sought to reaffirm requires that. My approach to these voices from the past, whoever they might be, is to let them say as much as they can, to allow them be my teachers, not to regard them simply as idols to be overthrown.

I believe that in the end an adequate psychology *of* women—that is, a psychology written *from* a female (and feminist) perspective—will be a psychology *about* and *for* all humans. Because I also believe that there must be a correspondence between means and end, it is my sense that if in the end we want to reinclude men, we need to do so at the beginning as well, we need to do so not just theoretically but concretely. This does not mean including them uncritically or sentimentally, but simply acknowledging: here Freud helps, here he hinders; here Jung sees, here he misperceives. This is not to ignore how the conventional interpretations of what such thinkers wrote about women has supported our misrepresentation and oppression, but rather to use every resource that might be available to help us frame a more adequate understanding.

I see us as offering midrashic interpretations of the received texts, as doing our own creative work in response to a past that changes, that is continually being rewritten. Because I appreciate the need for working in relation to a tradition, I feel I understand very well why Judith Plaskow remains a Jew who as a feminist must challenge almost every tenet of mainstream Judaic thought, why Elisabeth Schüssler Fiorenza and Rosemary Ruether have chosen to remain Christians yet devote themselves to radical re-formations of orthodox Catholic thought and practice. I haven't done that, probably because I never really *felt* my connection to a Jewish identity, which Hitler was far more ready to ascribe to me than was my half-Jewish father, and because the proclamation that Jesus was *the* son of God *never* made sense to me. But I have come to see how my pull to work out my own thinking through a never quite ending dialogue with Freud and Jung serves much the same function of discovering and highlighting the elements within a mostly male tradition that challenge patriarchy, that serve as "intimations of alternatives."[3]

Jung and *Freud*

Few feminists have spoken of finding Jung helpful in their search for a more adequate psychological theory, and until recently few female Jungian therapists or theorists acknowledged being dismayed or oppressed by the androcentric biases of archetypal psychology. Unfortunately there is still almost no mutual awareness between feminist and Jungian theorists; many Jungian women seem to be caught in a parochial isolation which keeps them unaware of the feminist revisionings of Freud, and most feminists are suspicious of Jung's disregard of human embodiment and historicity. Yet among the many antitheses that I feel we need to get beyond if we are to construct adequate psychologies of women is the one that says Freud *or* Jung.

I am struck by how few studies of Freud or Jung, by men or women, have pretended to an equal familiarity with the work of each or a genuine appreciation of both.[4] By now, it seems to me, we ought to be able to recognize the fruitfulness of the tensions between their thinking and to see that the differences between them are somewhat different from and more subtle than what either they or their followers have advertised. Important as Jung's misreading of Freud was to his own development, it is not a misreading in which we must participate. If we do, we are likely to misread Jung as much as we do Freud, by failing to recognize the degree to which he feels free (and perhaps obligated) to overemphasize certain aspects of his own thought because he knows that what he ignores is already powerfully being given its due by Freud. Nor do we need to reduce Freud to where he was at the time when they broke off all direct contact with one another and thus disregard the later works in which we find articulated some of the themes and perspectives we may have been accustomed to think of as "Jungian." The thinking of both is more dialectical and imaginative than that of the movements they spawned. As Paul Roazen's *Freud and His Followers* has helped us see, psychoanalysis has long since, though covertly, assimilated much in Jung's work that was once dismissed as deviant and heretical.[5] Freud deliberately invites us to search for the hidden, latent meanings of his thought; Jung encourages us to amplify his insights. My aim is to read both Freud and Jung in a way that allows both sets of motivations a full hearing. They present us with perspectives that complement one another but can no more be harmonized than can the two creation myths of Genesis. It is only when we read their psychologies literally that they seem grossly incompatible—and seem bad psychologies through which we can learn only what we already know.

I read Jung first and read Freud differently because of that. I have experienced Freud as the father over against whom I have developed some of my most important insights, Jung as the mother who brings me into renewing contact with the imaginal realm. I have felt the break between Freud and Jung as a divorce and find myself unwilling to choose one parent over against the other (as so many of their other children have felt they must). It is important to me to try to come to terms with both parents, not in order to reconcile them but to enable me to appropriate the full measure of what I inherit from each. It is congruent with this fantasy that I knew Jung's work long before I knew Freud's (as children, male and female alike, are intimate with the mother much earlier than with the father). My recognition of the close bond between myself and Jung was immediate and undeniable. He gave me myself: a vital, nourishing relationship to my inner life, my dreams and my image-making capabilities. But in time I felt too fascinated with the realm of images, absorbed by the all-embracing love of the Great Mother. Some spark necessary to my own standing apart was necessary. At this point I discovered Freud with whom there has never been the ease of relationship I knew with Jung. I have learned from Freud by contending with him and rebelling against him.

From my own experience I have come to appreciate the emphasis on the importance of triangles for psychic growth. As long as I can remember I have been intrigued with the myth of Persephone which illumines, among so much else, my relation to Freud and Jung. Like Hades, Freud intrudes between me and the mother figure. Persephone's separation from Demeter and from the maidens in the meadow is the necessary prelude to her discovery of her own identity. She comes to love her chthonic Zeus and yet also returns to spend part of each year with Demeter. Likewise I have come to recognize that my own vision needs to be continually mothered as well as fathered. Because these two speak to different sides of me, my bringing them together is necessary to my bringing these parts of myself together. The mother continues to be more seductive. Jung represents the pull to a language of mysticism, fantasy, image. Freud sometimes evokes in me a discourse that is overly literal, dogmatic, abstract. Really to relate to both leads to a different language—neither a sheer pouring forth of images nor a strictly denotative prose, but rather word tied to associative connections, to feelings, to temporal unfolding, that is the language of story and myth.

Freud was the daring but lonely first explorer who never forgot the fearsomeness of the new territory he had discovered and therefore often sought to protect himself with the armor of rationality. Many have seen only that armor. I know that my having known Jung first has helped me to see in Freud things many others don't, things which he himself at times denied.

Like many of the other feminists to whom I'll refer later in this chapter, I have found Freud's thinking about women more helpful to my own theorizing than Jung's. Nevertheless, I'm persuaded that there is much of value in Jung that we can't afford to jettison or ignore. My own notion of a *poetics* of the psyche is unimaginable apart from his influence.

Although I have many theoretical reservations about the details of his presentation, I continue to feel profound gratitude for the way Jung's theory of archetypes helps us—both personally and theoretically—to move beyond the limits of a psychology focused only on personal history and pathological issues. Archetypal images reveal a rich mirroring of our inner experience and our interactions with the world outside ourselves. As Jung discovered when he went in search of "the myth that was living him," the encounter with a dimension of the unconscious that is a living, creative, transpersonal source of inexhaustible energy and direction—and not merely repressed personal history—is life changing.

Many of us, when we first read Jung, feel we recognize immediately the dimension of experience for which he used the word "archetypal." I remember very well my own first reading when I was in my early twenties and imagined myself as fully and fulfillingly defined by the roles of wife and mother. Suddenly my self-understanding was opened up as I began to pay attention to dreams which introduced me to an unsuspected multitude of unlived potentialities waiting to be acknowledged and nurtured. I discovered also how these roles themselves had archetypal and numinous dimensions (both threatening and life-giving) to which I had been blinded by my involvement with their more trivial aspects. I felt myself in touch with elements of my own experience that were not mine alone. The recognition that I shared my deepest feelings, my most profound hopes and fears, my most valued accomplishments and most regretted failures with others gave me an entirely new sense of being connected to all humanity not just through outward relationships but at the very core of my being.

Lou Salome thanked Freud for giving her much the same gift that I feel I received from Jung:

> Perhaps it is precisely within the sphere of psychoanalytical thought (which you have revealed to us) that one feels most profoundly that each person endures everything for all the others and that no experience is ever wasted, but remains a permanent help and assurance. I was not formerly aware of this in any way; now I know it—I would like to think—for ever.[6]

My experience felt transformative. Jung had introduced me to a new world and, more importantly, to a truly new vision of myself which I recognized as both liberating and challenging.

When Jung spoke of the images through which the collective unconscious manifests itself as "archetypal," he meant to communicate their power to bring us in touch with what feels like the very source of our being. Jung recognized that what comes into individual consciousness are always *archetypal images*, particular, concrete manifestations influenced by sociocultural and individual factors. Archetypes themselves are formless and unrepresentable, *psychoid*, rather than, properly speaking, *psychic.*

Jung's interest in archetypal images reflects his emphasis on the *form* of unconscious thought rather than on the content. Our capacity to respond to experience as image-making creatures is, he believed, inherited, given to us with our humanness. Archetypal images are not remnants of archaic thought, not dead deposits, but part of a living system of interactions between the human psyche and the outer world. The archetypal images that appear in our dreams spring from the same human capacity that gave rise to ancient mythologies among our remote ancestors. The myths are not causes of the contemporary and individual manifestations, but rather exist on the same plane, as analogies.

The focus on the archetypal emphasizes the importance of our images in making us who we are. Our thoughts and deeds, and, even more powerfully, our fantasies and dreams, and the complex feeling-toned associations with which we respond to the persons and events that we encounter in our daily lives, these all shape our lives. I am not merely what I have thought, as Descartes proposed, nor simply what I have done, as the existentialists claim, but also, as Gaston Bachelard has so powerfully shown, what I have imagined and remembered.[7]

It is important to recognize that when he speaks of archetypal images, Jung is not referring simply to dream images, or to mythological or literary images. He is speaking of a way of responding to our ordinary lives with our imaginations, rather than only pragmatically or logically, of a way of being in the world that is open to many dimensions of meaning, open to resonances, echoes, to associative and synchronous connections, not only causal ones. He is speaking of a world discovered to be full of sign-ificance— of signs, symbols, metaphors, images.

Thus the point of attending to the archetypal is to bring us to appreciate and nurture the natural, spontaneous human capacity to respond to the world symbolically, not only conceptually. For Jung this capacity for symbol making, not reason, is the truly human-making function. Attending to these images (which are not translated ideas but the natural speech of the soul, its authentic *logos*) helps get us beyond the tyranny of the verbal and rational modes, which have issued in the suppression of those human faculties we encounter as "unconscious."

When we focus on the archetypal *image*, it becomes clear that there is no absolute distinction between the personal and the collective; the archetypal image marks the juncture where inner and outer, personal and collective meet. It represents the continual dynamic interaction between the conscious and the unconscious, the personal and the collective.

I do not believe that archetypal images *are* a priori, universal, or numinous—but that part of their power comes from our *feeling* that they are.

Archetypal images feel basic and necessary and generative. They are connected to something *original*, not in the sense of what they are caused by but, rather, in what they help to cause or make possible. They seem to give energy and direction. Archetypal images are generative; they give rise to associations, lead us to other images, because we experience them as having resonance, complexity, depth.

They feel *universal*. Though I question the accuracy (or even the relevance) of the claim to literal universality, I nonetheless believe that the sense of being in touch with something that feels collective, shared, is indeed part of what "archetypal" connotes.

Archetypal images feel *objective,* not dependent on prior personal experience, not explicable on the basis of our conscious knowledge. We are often amazed to discover parallels between the images and motifs which seem to have spontaneously appeared in our own dreams and those which figure prominently in myths or folktales we knew nothing about. The impact of these correspondences is powerful, quite independent of how we might be tempted to explain (or explain away) such coincidences.

These images feel deep, *numinous*, magic, fascinating, daemonic or divine. The images feel as though they have a *transcendent,* autonomous source, beyond individual consciousness, beyond ourselves. There is a dangerous aspect to this feeling, the danger of being inflated or possessed, the danger of taking this to mean that in some way these images are sacred and thus inviolable, unchangeable, that they come endowed with a cosmic endorsement.[8]

All archetypal images seem to evoke *ambivalence* in us. We are drawn to them and repelled by them; they have their dark, fearsome, destructive aspects, as well as a benign, creative side. We often try to deny this, to emphasize only the creative aspect, or to moralize and divide the archetype into good and bad parts— the positive mother, the negative mother, for example— and thereby lose some of the dynamic energy intrinsic to the images.

They feel *transformative*. Jung always emphasized that archetypal images are connected to future as well as past:

> The self . . . not only contains the deposit and totality of all past life, but is also a point of departure, the fertile soil from which all future life will spring. This premonition of futurity is as clearly impressed upon our innermost feelings as is the historical aspect.[9]

He warns against taking this teleological aspect literally. We are not to think of archetypal images as having a ready-made meaning, but as pointers; otherwise, we degrade them to being the mental equivalents of fortune-tellers. The images are rather to be understood as presenting us with lifelines to be followed provisionally, for "life does not follow lines that are straight, nor lines whose course can be seen far in advance."[10]

It remains important, however, to recall that *we* give archetypal images this value, this significance. We are so easily led to reify, hypostasize, to separate the archetype from the psyche, to act as though we could freeze the ever-changing context in which the images appear.

There is no, can be no, definitive list of archetypes or archetypal images. After his break with Freud, Jung spoke of going in search of *the* myth that was living him, but actually our lives are shaped by a *plurality* of archetypal images. To be informed by only one is to be in its thrall and to abdicate the living tension of their interplay. For the many different images do not always arrange themselves in a neatly ordered hierarchical pantheon. Often, we will find them to be in conflict, painful conflict, with one another.

Jung always recognized the importance of conscious active involvement with the archetypal images, of opening up a true dialogue between consciousness and the unconscious. This entails neither repudiating nor identifying with the image—or with the ego. The point of conscious engagement with archetypal images is not to strengthen the ego, but rather to relativize it, to come to see that ego, too, is an archetype. The archetypal perspective liberates us from viewing the ego's perspective as the only one. An archetypal view is inherently pluralistic, polytheistic, and thus inevitably critical of the dominance of the psyche by ego, hero, king, father, as it is suspicious of an unquestioning valorization of the goals of autonomy, integration, wholeness, growth. The very notion of archetype challenges the supremacy of the conscious, literal, fixed, linear, abstract mind.

The point of archetypal images, like the point of myths, is not problem solving but "imagining, questioning, going deeper."[11] The point is to activate the imagination, to free us from identifying ourselves with our literal failures and successes, or from seeing our lives as only banal or trivial. The aim in attending to these images is to awaken us to a sense of our yet unrealized latent possibilities, to save us from our sense of isolation and meaninglessness, from loneliness, confusion, and joylessness. The purpose is to open up our lives to renewal and reshaping.

Attending to the archetypal images creates a new bond between our personal lives and the collective experience of humankind. This accounts for the liberating effect to which so many people can testify. As Jung said:

> Life is crazy and meaningful at once. And when we do not laugh over the one aspect and speculate about the other, life is exceedingly drab, and everything is reduced to the littlest scale. There is then little sense and little nonsense either.[12]

What Jung contributes to my articulations of a psychology of women is then not really anything he writes about women per se, but rather an encouragement to amplify, to honor soul, depth, numinosity, to take time to reflect, to value the language of image rather than abstract language, to stay close to my own experience, to be taught by my dreams. Jung helps me recognize the ongoing dynamic interchange between conscious and unconscious processes, helps me remember that by "unconscious" we mean a symbolic, associational mode of consciousness that can be activated in waking life, and that connects us to the future as well as the past. Above all, Jung has given me access to a different view of Freud than I might otherwise have.

A Herstory of Psychology

To exorcise the inadequate ways in which depth psychology has described women and to prepare for the creation of more adequate ways require a review of the history —beginning with Freud *and* Jung and then examining the very gradual process through which women have come to be not just the objects of psychological inquiry but also active, innovative, persuasive subjects. My history proceeds by way of an admittedly somewhat artificial typology but one which I nevertheless hope will help us see an important pattern of development. What it fails adequately to take into account is how much the old ways of looking still persist, how much of the new remains unheard, and how even the earliest voices have not really been silenced or overcomne, how they, too, may still have new things to say. It also may misleadingly ignore the degree to which changes within the field have been stimulated by external factors, by larger sociocultural events and by individual life stories. I review the history to help me place myself as its heir.

Depth psychology has from its beginnings recognized that the psychology of women is in some way the clue to an adequate psychology of the human. Indeed, there is a sense in which we might say that depth psychology was discovered by a woman, by Breuer's famous patient "Anna O." (Bertha Pappenheim), who in the early 1880s (a few years before Esther Harding was born) invented the "talking cure," and went on to become an articulate and powerful feminist whose energies were devoted to working with abused children and battered women.[13]

Still, we know her primarily as the first psychoanalytical *patient*, and it is as patients that women enter depth psychology. Women enter psychology as objects not subjects, as in science generally the knower has been male, the known conceived in female terms.[14] Knowing has traditionally been construed as "male" performance; to be female is to be passive, the object known rather than the knowing subject.

Freud, to a greater degree than is always recognized, began a move beyond this perspective. He sought to attend to the *psyche-logos*, the speech of the soul, of the female hysterics who were his first patients. He listened to them and was able to hear in their symptoms an unconscious protest at the social limitations imposed on them by virtue of their gender. Nevertheless, Freud was clearly interpreting the experience of these women from his own male perspective. In his early writings he defined woman as a deviation from the male norm, as a deficient, castrated male. His later writings show him recognizing the inadequacy of assuming a simple parallelism between male and female development, the fallacy (for example) of deducing that the male Oedipus complex implies a female Electra complex. Freud came to appreciate the central importance of a young girl's pre-Oedipal attachment to her mother, to the *same*-sex parent, and to admit how little a male analyst can learn about the deepest strata of female experience because of the unlikelihood of his inspiring a fully articulated mother transference. Freud began to glimpse the asymmetry—and the mystery.

Jung also began with male experience and extrapolated from it in constructing his psychology of women. That Jung has so much positive to say about the "feminine," about receptivity, feeling, intuition, the aptitude for relationship he calls Eros—and writes so eloquently about the limitations of the "masculine" reliance on "Logos" and outward achievement—may keep us from noticing how smoothly he elides the distinction between "feminine" and "female." He assumes that he can know the "feminine" by consulting his own experience, male experience. He takes for granted that masculine and feminine are complementary realities, and like Freud often writes in a way that implies an endorsement of conventional femininity as an appropriate norm and ideal for contemporary women.

Jung's own most disconcerting experiences had led him to a hitherto unconscious aspect of his psyche which presented itself as contrasexual, as feminine, an aspect which he came to call the *anima*. On the basis of this powerful personal engagement he inferred the centrality of contrasexuality in the inner life of all of us. Both men and women, he believed, come to learn who they are through contact with an inner contrasexual other. For men the relation to their unconscious femininity, to their anima, is a relationship to their own lost, longed-for wholeness, to their soul.

Jung understands very well how a man's relationship to actual women can be contaminated by projection of this unconscious aspect of themselves. He sees less clearly the degree to which his psychology of women is a projection onto women of a male psychology. He fails to see anything problematical in deducing that the mirror image of what is true of men is true of women. It seems obvious to him that if men have an anima, women will have an *animus*, an unconscious masculine side. Jung says explicitly that this is an inference, that the notion of the animus did not derive from the testimony of his women patients. Indeed, he acknowledges that these women often could not understand the concept nor accept its relevance to their own experience.[15] Nevertheless, Jung held it as self-evident that for women as for men an inner contrasexual reality mediates the relation to the Self.

Jung could work with his culture's conventional definitions of gender and at the same time take account of their felt inadequacy to the self-understanding and experience of individuals. He could regard gender as necessarily and appropriately defining ego-consciousness: males are masculine in their ego-orientation as females are feminine. He could safely assume that he and his contemporaries had a shared understanding of what masculinity and femininity imply. These attributes could be taken to have permanant, universal and transcultural connotations. Jung seems persuaded that, at least for the ego, anatomy is fate. Perhaps because of his relative lack of interest in the details of personal history or the specifics of acculturation, he was able to view his own society's definition of "masculinity" and "femininity" as archetypal. This was, no doubt, facilitated by his looking at gender not in terms of sexual interaction or social role but rather as referring primarily to psychical attributes. "Masculine" means rational, extroverted, active, as "feminine" means introverted, receptive, in touch with feeling, adept at intimate relationship.

Yet Jung goes on to acknowledge that this gendered definition is woefully deficient as a description of the whole of any individual's psyche. Each of us, he believes, carries the other gender's psychical attributes in our unconscious (as *anima* or *animus)* and are wounded, incomplete, until (or unless) we come to recognize this unknown other within as part of ourselves. Given his sense of a self-evident difference between masculinity and femininity, Jung believed one could clearly distinguish between this inner contrasexual element and what he calls the "shadow," a same-sex inner alter ego which carries all our disavowed personal history. The shadow, too, needs to be integrated, but that is a preliminary task. It is anima and animus that provide access to the creative depths of the psyche.

Thus for Jung the goal of individuation, the process of realizing our potential wholeness, is androgyny. Coming to terms with gender involves primarily an *inner* struggle whose aim is harmonious complementation of one's feminine and masculine aspects. Engagement with anima or animus makes possible a withdrawal of projections from members of the other sex from whom we may have expected an easement of our own incompleteness that can truly only come from within.

This then makes possible a different kind of interpersonal relationship. "Even the hermaphrodite needs the human other," Jung says[16]—but for that hermaphrodite presumably the gender of the other is essentially irrelevant. Or, rather, now gender difference means not a one-sided psychical orientation but simply sexual difference—a difference to be enjoyed not overcome. His emphasis, however, always falls on the achievement of a harmonious inner relationship between ego and anima, ego and animus, on what he calls the *mysterium coniunctionis* or the *hieros gamos.* On what I call the fairy-tale ending: they lived happily ever after.

Gender seemed less problematic then, half a century ago, in part because it was defined from a single point of view. Many of the limitations of Jung's theory derive not simply from its having been framed in another time but from its having been constructed so exclusively from a male perspective.

To see female experience as but a simple inversion of male experience (if men have an anima, it follows that women have an animus) presumes that men can understand women on the basis of their own experience without needing to consult women themselves. This suggestsd that men can understand women as well as they understand themselves, indeed that women may need the help of men to achieve self-understanding. The *logos* requisite to theoretical construction is taken to be a masculine attribute to which women rarely have access as a conscious function. So women need men and femininity requires complementation by masculinity. That, however, is only half the story. When this understanding of female psychology is combined with the Jungian notion that men have an inner feminine aspect, there is a subtle insinuation that individuated men can be as feminine as women, that women exist primarily to help men toward their femininity, and that ultimately men don't need women. The unspoken (and, no doubt, when formulated, unconscious) message is that women need men and men don't need women—a message which may owe its urgency to its being the obverse of an older and deeper truth, that men depend on female birth givers for their very being-here. Nonetheless, for a long while it is the message about male self-sufficiency and superiority which has been in force.

Thus both Freud (especially in his earlier writings) and Jung offer us androcentric psychologies. Both assume that male experience is normative for human experience. They look upon female experience as an inference from, a variation of, male experience. They see nothing problematic in their roles as interpreters, definers, nor in their consignment of women to the role of the defined, the objectified.

Not too surprisingly, when the objectified began to speak on their own behalf, they spoke *as* the objectified, the defined. When in the 1920s women like Marie Bonaparte and Helene Deutsch became analysts and began to write about the psychology of women, they initially tried to fit their experience within the framework provided by male theorists — even when the lack of fit between theory and experience seems to have required as radical a self-mutilation as that of Cinderella's sisters cutting at heels and toes in order to fit their feet into the golden slipper. (As Simone de Beauvoir understood, there may be secondary gains involved in accepting the role of the objectified, the other; there is something in all human beings that would welcome being defined and happily accept being let off from the responsibility of self-definition.) Celia Bertin's biography of Bonaparte shows the events in Bonaparte's childhood and early adulthood that may help us understand how she became a spokeswoman for the idea that true femininity requires overcoming one's fear of pain and penetration, accepting the role of erotic passivity, and learning to get pleasure from submission. Deutsch's autobiography and Paul Roazen's recent study make more comprehensible how this career-focused woman came to identify femininity with motherhood to such an extravagant degree and why she believed that we women need men to initiate us into knowledge of our own sexuality.[17]

Gradually, beginning in the early 1930s, women became more conscious of the oppression inherent in having their psychology defined by men. Karen Horney, having seen that "until now the psychology of women has been a deposit of the desires and disappointments of men," decided to begin with the actual experience of female children in constructing her own psychology of women. She found not penis envy but fear of penetration, an awareness of female physical vulnerability. Indeed, she came to believe that the real envy determinative of human psychology is male womb envy. The secret dread of women felt by men leads, she believes, to a reactive assertion of male power and the establishment of societies where penis envy (as signifying woman's envy of men's social power) is realistic.[18]

Horney's contemporary, Clara Thompson, too, insists that penis envy is a social not a biological or archetypal reality; women are not castrated males but they are disenfranchised human beings. Recognizing the social construction of gender, she asserts that we can have no knowledge of what "femaleness" is apart from what culture has made it. Her writings communicate real appreciation for the many different forms that women's lives may take—none ipso facto "normal" or "pathological," and none fully satisfying.[19]

The move in the direction of taking on the subject role proceeded more slowly among Jungians, perhaps because Jung's oft voiced appreciation of the "feminine" masked the androcentric bias of his theory. Though Toni Wolff sought to distinguish the feminine in women from the feminine in men, each of her "four forms of the Feminine" is primarily defined in terms of a particular way women may relate to men.[20] Emma Jung's study of the animus[21] provides a subtle, complex rendering of how the animus in the form of internalized male voices may encourage women's self-denigration, but she never directly considers that the animus as a theoretical construct might serve an analogous function. I noted earlier how Harding, despite her genuinely original perspective, abstained from any direct challenge to Jungian theory.

Only in the 1950s did a Jungian, Marie Louise von Franz, look directly at the difference between the feminine in men and actual women. She argued that Apuleius's fairy tale about Amor and Psyche (which Erich Neuman had interpreted as representing the female journey toward Self) was to be understood as a reflection of male involvement with the anima. What she saw made visible in the tale was a man (whether Apuleius himself or his protagonist, Lucian, or perhaps both) attempting to integrate the feminine, not a woman devoting herself to the individuation process.[22] In many of her other writings von Franz clearly indicates how differently we will understand a myth or fairy tale depending on whether we read its female characters as representing an aspect of the male or the female psyche.

Even more innovative was Irene Claremont de Castillejo's admission (in an essay found among her papers after her death) that she had come to recognize that neither her own experience nor that of her female patients was really adequately described by Jung's animus theory. The "soul images of women," she had discovered, were female not male images. De Castillejo proposed no alternative theory. Indeed, she seemed to doubt whether women are capable of the kind of comprehensive abstract thinking requisite for theory construction. In any case, believing that new theory making would be premature, she proposed that our re-visioning begin at the phenomenological level, that we should begin by gathering women's own uninterpreted accounts of their dreams and other powerful imaginal experiences. Yet she did hint at the possibility of a new kind of theory, less abstract and less normative than the one she had inherited.[23]

Beginning in the 1950s with the publication of Simone de Beauvoir's *The Second Sex*, and continuing more vociferously in the 1960s, women became more conscious of the patriarchal biases of the depth psychological tradition and of the costs of their own co-optation by these theories. No longer content to be defined as "the other," they claimed the right to speak for themselves, and thereby fully to take on the subject role. They articulated their recognition of the *formative* (and not simply descriptive) power of theory in such slogans as The Personal Is the Political.

The first rereadings of Freud from a feminist perspective (Kate Millett's, for example[24]) were angry—and simplistic. Freud's descriptions of female psychology were rejected entirely, in part because there was no attempt to sort out descriptive from prescriptive statements, in part because there was no attempt to distinguish what Freud himself had written from what his admirers and detractors took him to have said. Though these critiques may seem exaggerated in retrospect, my sense is that in their own time they were appropriate. They brought vividly into view the egregious effects of the equation of difference with inferiority that had permeated so many of the "classical" texts.

These first articulations of a self-consciously feminist approach to the psychology of women were cast in the rhetoric of protest. There was little attempt to define what female experience looks like from a female perspective. Rather, there were global affirmations to the effect that there are no real differences between men and women (only patriarchally constructed ones) *or* that there are enormous differences, but not the ones described by males—for in a matriarchal world women were (and could again be) unwounded and unwounding.

A decade later it was possible (often with reference to the work of Jacques Lacan) to reread psychoanalysis in a more subtle and appreciative way. Juliet Mitchell understood Freud as providing us with access to some painful truths about women's lives in patriarchal societies. She read what Freud had written about the woundedness of women in the context of what he had written about the woundedness of all who live under "The Law of the Father."[25] Reminding us of Freud's emphasis on the power of *unconscious* attitudes, she made evident how the misogyny of our culture resides not just in its institutions but deep in our psyches —even in the psyches of women who at a conscious, political level see sisterhood as powerful and beautiful.

The first explicitly feminist critique of Jung was published by Naomi Goldenberg just a few years after Mitchell's ground-breaking work. Goldenberg criticized Jung's sexism and essentialism, his stereotypical notions of masculine and feminine, and his focus on archetypes as unchanging, universal, transcendent ideals. Jung deemed it "unnatural" for women not to live in accord with the feminine archetype. Goldenberg saw this as setting arbitrary limitations on the development of both sexes and reinforcing oppressive stereotypes.[26]

More recently, there has been a great outburst of innovative writing about women in Jungian circles, although most of it is not consciously radical. Many female analysts have sought to fill out traditional Jungian theory by paying attention to the particularities of women's own dreams and experiences and by exploring the contemporary resonance of archaic and traditional woman-centered myth and ritual, rather than by engaging in a fundamental recasting of the theory. At the same time, some academic scholars, less tied to the day-by-day demands of clinical practice—for instance, Estella Lauter, Carole Rupprecht, Demaris Wehr —have initiated a more critical revisioning of Jungian theory, particularly as it applies to women.

Beyond Psychology

Recently feminists have begun to see that the patriarchal biases of psychological theory affect the whole value system of psychology, not only its view of women. When male experience is taken as the norm for human experience, everything will be out of balance. As Carol Gilligan so plainly says, when a theory does not fit women, it may be because of weaknesses inherent in the theory. Gilligan proposed that if the application of an understanding of human maturity (such as Kohlberg's) discovers that women rarely attain the highest level of maturity, there may be something wrong with the very definition of maturity being employed. This led her to a radical questioning of whether the valorization of autonomy and of abstract thinking that underlies Kohlberg's definition really constitutes a satisfactorily complex view of moral maturity.[27]

Her work helped bring into view how dominated psychological theory has been by abstract and normative thinking—not just in its contents but in its structure. As women have begun to ask why psychological theory has been so based on antithetical thinking, so obsessed with dualities and polarities, with hierarchies and norms, so committed to objectivity and abstraction, they have discovered that the high value placed on this style of thinking seems to be connected to some particularities of male infantile development.

Most recently women have been engaged in interpreting the objectification, in trying to understand what creates and sustains patriarchal culture. They are finding Freud, especially the late Freud's writings about the relationship between the mother and the pre-Oedipal daughter, an important resource in their re-interpretation. They are interested in the reproduction of gender, in how the discovery of gender identity seems to be correlative with the beginnings of consciousness and with the discovery of the difference between self and other —which is initially primarily the discovery of the difference between self and mother. For the female child, they suggest, this involves a discovery of separateness but likeness; for the male, a discovery not only of separateness but of otherness, dissimilarity—a more radical kind of difference. The boy's response expresses a highly charged ambivalence—a *wish*, a longing *not* to be different and separate, but also a *fear*, an anxiety about losing what sets him apart, what gives him his identity. The discovery of being male is in the first instance a discovery of *not* being female—and thus a discovery of contingency, vulnerability, finitude, mortality.

Both Dorothy Dinnerstein and Nancy Chodorov have written with compelling insight and real compassion about how naturally this leads males to hold on to what sets them apart, their maleness, and to accord it high value. This in turn leads to a valorization of separation and autonomy, achievement and "world making," the abstract and rational, the permanent and the stable. They describe a pattern whereby males learn who they are as males through the painful experience of a more exaggerated separation from their mother than that experienced by females—and then repress or turn upside down that original experience of difference. Where at first "male" means "not female," being male comes to be redefined as being human and then females are redescribed as deficient males. The difference is rediscovered, objectified, and viewed in a highly polarized and hierarchical way.[28]

I find this way of looking at female and male development insightful and yet am also aware of some limitations. Primarily, I find the theory too sociological, too literal, too in a sense *uninformed* by Freud's most important contribution, his "discovery" of the unconscious. For Chodorov and other American feminists working in the object-relations tradition seem to presuppose what they are trying to explain—the production of gender identity. The emphasis on "likeness" and "unlikeness" implies that gender is based on anatomical sex. Whereas the French feminist deconstructionists may engage in a dizzying disappearing act with gender, the Americans may somewhat naively grant it too much unproblematic solidity. They seem to forget we are reflecting on ways of *imaging* a relationship and to forget it may be imagined otherwise. As Butler observes, the focus on maternal identification comes to occupy a hegemonic position within feminist theory and reinforces the binary heterosexist framework even as it tries to explain it.[29] Thus Chodorov's "creation myth" has no good way of accounting for male homosexuality.[30] There is room for only one story, one predetermined script.

Perhaps because psychological theory has until recently been written almost entirely from a male perspective, it has incorporated the abstract, antithetical, normative style. We are just beginning to explore what a psychological theory that would instead begin with female experience might look like. As one in love with language and linguistic roots, I cannot help but hear in our word "theory" the Greek *theoria*; I cannot help but remember that our word "theater" comes from the same root and that originally theory meant *vision*. Thus my understanding of theory is deeply informed by the Socratic model: by the testimony of the Platonic dialogues that the deepest theoretical insights can only be communicated in imaginal, poetic, mythological language; by their evidence that theory can only be created communally, dialogically, in the presence of Eros. There are aspects of female experience that suggest to me that this model of theorizing may be especially congenial to us.

According to the object-relations perspective, the female child's early experience vis-à-vis the mother makes separation from her, a same-sex other, less traumatic, less exaggerated. Women learn early that one can be other without being opposite, that there are subtle degrees of difference. They experience early that one can be close without being merged. The different early experience suggests the possibility of being more comfortable with less objectifying modes of thought than the subject-object model allows for. I can see how women may more easily move beyond the traditional reliance on abstract language as the only language appropriate in theoretical discourse, may more readily use the language of image and myth (though Freud and Jung were obviously precursors here). Women may be less likely to regard the abstract archetype as more "real" than the directly appearing image. We may find it more natural to value difference and variety, to avoid the language of norms and of pathology. It may not be quite as difficult for us to speak in the first person, to speak of our own experience and not just about others, to speak from the experience of woundedness and objectification.

As in our thinking about psyche-logos we rediscover that knower and known are alike, that we are speaking of the psyche's knowledge of the psyche, we see that we are moving toward a knowledge that is not objective but erotic. We know psyche, our own and one another's, by participation and by analogy. I believe it important to apply this to our theory of theory construction. My hope is that as women begin to create theory, we will do it through dialogue, through sharing our experience and our ideas, that we will not expect agreement nor grant any one perspective authoritative power.

I see us as moving past what we might call a "heterosexual" model of knowledge, a model which emphasizes the otherness of subject and object. I believe we must also move beyond the parental model of knowledge or, more specifically, beyond a theory written from the perspective of sons who fear being swallowed by the mother or see themselves as in competition with the father, and who therefore see all knowledge not only in terms of objective distancing but also in terms of domination and control. I suspect a daughter-based psychology has its dangers also, the dangers Dinnerstein mentions of being transfixed by the dream of a conflict-free world ruled by an all-giving and all-powerful mother.

The psychology I imagine as emerging from female experience would entail our recognizing that mothers, too, are daughters, are vulnerable and needy like ourselves—are *sisters.* That is, I envision a psychology of sisters—and brothers. I recall here some lines from Rilke's *Letters to a Young Poet*:

> Perhaps the sexes are more akin than people think, and the
> great renewal of the world will perhaps consist in one phenom-

enon: that man and woman, freed from all mistaken feelings and aversions, will seek each other out not as opposites but as brother and sister, as neighbors, and will unite as *human beings*, in order to bear in common, simply, earnestly, and patiently, the heavy sex that has been laid upon them.[31]

Obviously I am not talking about simply a different psychology *about* women. The new psychologies of women I have in mind (and I expect there will be many of them, not all in obvious harmony with one another) would be psychologies put forward *by* women about the *human*.

The traditional model distorts male experience, not only female experience, and it exaggerates the differences between men and women. Yet to avoid the trap of perpetuating antithetical thinking is an enormously difficult task in a culture so pervasively based on it. We need to remember not to identify men with that which seems to distinguish them from women—and to remember, also, that we women, too, are drawn to create and to transform, to participate in what Dinnerstein calls "world making." All of us, men and women, need to move beyond the belief that fusion or domination/submissions are the only alternatives. All of us need to recognize how our human identification of knowledge as control has come to threaten all human life and perhaps all life on this planet. A new psychology of women would, I believe, move not only to a new understanding of the human and of our interdependence with one another—but beyond that, to a recognition of our interdependence with all that lives. And if it is true that separation is a less intense need for women, we may not need to insist as much as men often have on the separation of psyche from body or the human from the natural.

Thus I am really talking about a psychology "beyond psychology." The term is Otto Rank's but I mean by it even more than did he.[32] Rank spoke of psychoanalysis as "the last strand of patriarchy," as a *logos* designed to control the irrational, even though we actually cannot help but *live* irrationally. By going beyond psychology he meant learning to live beyond the accepted psychology, finding a way of balancing our longing for control with a more receptive, yielding attitude. He believed that Freud, Jung, and Adler had all seen the pain caused by bourgeois culture's emphasis on individual autonomy, but not recognized that the only remedy lay in moving beyond a psychology based on the individual. Freud's recognition of the importance of moving from narcissistic self-preoccupation to erotic involvement did not, Rank believed, state clearly enough how our fear of submission masks our *need* of another, our need to *be* loved. Rank believed that misogyny, the fear and hatred of women, expresses men's fear of all otherness and their refusal of mortality. To move beyond psychology is to move beyond the individual through love. "The psychology of the Self is to be found in the Other," he says.

Rank also saw the need for first stepping beyond language as men have spoken it in order to move beyond psychology. Indeed, he had an intimation that women's language about the psyche would be different, though he left it to us to discover and make manifest *how* different.[33]

Many of my themes are reiterations of his—and I am grateful for his encouraging women to create a new language that might enable us to articulate our psychology beyond psychology.

I look toward a psychology that recognizes the importance of our relationship to our bodies, to human others, to human history (including the history of social oppression), and to the natural world. The new theory, the new vision, must be created out of love, out of a sense of our likenesses and an appreciation of our differences.

The revisioned, newly visioned, psychology I imagine is inspired by a love of the human race—by a love of women and of men, by a real sense of our shared fragility and of our beautiful but also destructive human pull to achieve, create, change. It emerges out of a love of the natural world, and out of a recognition that it is imperative that we now exorcise the fears that issued in our objectification of one another, the fears that helped shape the old psychology of women—for unless we do so, those same fears may destroy our planet.

·4·

BODY AND SOUL

Women's mysteries in the ancient world recalled the sacredness of specifically female modes of existence. Although each of the Greek goddesses had both male and female devotees, there were also rituals associated with each open only to women. Each goddess was recognized as relevant to particular aspects of female experience.

Among the Greek goddesses Artemis is the one most identified with the mysteries of the female body and the one most dedicated to an all-women's sociability; she shuns the world of men and spends her time in the wilderness either alone or in the company of other females, the nymphs. She is a lady of the wild things, including the instinctual wildness within herself. She teaches her worshipers to know their body, their feeling, their desire as their own. The mysteries dedicated to Artemis were specifically focused on celebrating the sacral significance of those aspects of female experience connected to the particularities of female physiology: the onset of menstruation, the loss of virginity, the discovery of one's own sexual passion, the potential for loss of the claim to one's body as one's own inherent in marriage, the bodily changes associated with conception, childbirth, nursing, menopause, and, ultimately, with death.

To honor Artemis is to engage in close attending to what our female bodies can teach us (or remind us) of what being a woman is all about. She encourages us to explore the complex, subtle interrelations between body and psyche, the soul meaning of gendered embodiment.

This is, I well understand, a problematic beginning point. Women have so often been identified with body and nature, and this identification has then so often been used as an excuse to view us as inferior to spirit-oriented, culture-minded men, and as a rationale for confining us to our procreative capacity. So much of feminist theorizing and politicking in the last decades has been dedicated to challenging that identification. Why should I now seek to reinstate it?

The answer is, of course, that I don't. Women and men are equally embodied, equally imbedded in nature, equally capable of cultural achievement, of "world making." Nonetheless, there are aspects of female physiology which may make us women a little less likely to disown our embodiment, a little more likely to remember our connection to nature.

I recognize that we women may seem to be playing once again a foreordained role if we now emerge as spokespersons on behalf of the body and the natural—and so, of course, we are tempted to resist taking on that charge. But somebody has to! Not for the sake of proving or disproving any theory about women and nature—but for the sake of the continuation of life on this planet. We humans are all equally connected to the natural world and those among us who remember our interconnectedness recognize the necessity of reminding the rest of us.

Anatomy and Destiny

When Freud said that anatomy is destiny, he meant primarily that our bodies remind us of our finitude and our inescapable connection to the instinctual, the natural. While to speak of anatomy as *fate* implies that our biology irrevocably and inevitably causally shapes our lives or at least defines the "natural" and "right" shaping of them, to see anatomy as *destiny* means recognizing that our bodies provide us with some "givens," but that what we do with these possibilities and limitations is open. "Destiny" (which has the same root as "destination") connotes teleological rather than effective causality. It implies a notion of purpose and goal and a recognition of the relevance of the intentions with which we respond to the bodies we are given. "Fate" is often associated with an adverse outcome, whereas destiny usually has a more benign connotation. Thus to speak in terms of "destiny" rather than "fate" implies a move from a biological to a more psychological understanding of embodiment.

Our complex Western notions of fate and destiny derive primarily from early Greek conceptions. The Greek word *moira* (often but somewhat misleadingly translated as "fate") originally meant simply one's "portion" or "lot" in life. Not only humans but even the Olympian gods (who after all were not cosmogonic divinities but rather late arrivals in a world already made) have their allotted portion: Zeus, Poseidon, and Hades, for example, are assigned their specific spheres of influence by lot.

Originally *moira* was taken to refer to the distinctive events of an individual's life, especially to the particular character of one's death, whether due to natural causes or some divine decree. Only after the fourth century B.C.E. did *moira* come to be viewed as a general scheme ruling the world at large and circumscribing the whole life of an individual. Thus In Homer *moira* refers to what interrupts the normal course of human life and is specific to the individual, signifying not the working out of a general plan, not the sum of a life, but rather only what appears like a sudden reversal, particularly an unexpected violent death.[1]

Elsewhere in Greek literature we find not the impersonal *moira* but three personified *Moirae* who in later poetry are even named: Lachesis, Clotho, and Atropos. The *Moirae* are most often imagined as spinning a thread around an individual as around a spindle, though sometimes they are said to sing our lives rather than spin them and in Ovid they write their decrees. Some texts suggest that they finish their spinning at birth, others that it continues throughout an individual's life. Sometimes the spinning work of Lachesis is seen as completed at the time of our birth, the invisible binding attributed to Clotho (analogous, Richard Onions suggests, to our sense of what is *bound* to happen) as persisting through one's life, and the final binding at death worked by Atropos as irreversible. The spun threads are gifts given at birth. During one's lifetime the binding might be unloosed, much as Penelope can undo her weaving. Thus Homer represents Zeus as wanting to unbind Patroclus and Hector from the doom with which they have been bound—but because the allotting is associated with an ordered, proper, right world, he finds himself restrained (morally not physically restrained) from doing so. Dionysos, on the other hand, because not so constrained, is known as the "loosing God."[2]

In Homer not surprisingly the *Moirae* are subordinate to Zeus and even Hesiod in one passage of the *Theogony* describes them as children of Zeus and his first consort, Themis, the Titan daughter of Gaia who represents the moral order of the universe—though elsewhere Hesiod says that the *Moirae* are the offspring of Night.[3] Later, the Orphics and Pythagoreans view them as daughters of *Ananke*, Necessity.

Like the *Erinyes*, the underworld powers who punish those who violate the matristic order, the *Moirae* were probably already present in the prepatriachal matristic world. They are associated with all the great realities of life, death, and other troubles, but also with propitious moments, with birth, weddings, riches, and homecomings. Like the Latin *Parcae* they may originally have been deities of childbearing and birth, particularly associated with beginnings and thus with births and marriages. On their wedding day brides offered cuttings of their hair to the *Moirae*; when their labors were difficult, young mothers called upon them for help. Like Eilytheia, the childbirth goddess among the Olympians, they are goddesses who bring gifts to the newborn. There is evidence that as birth goddesses the *Moirae* were even invoked to bless the fields.

The *Moirae* are closely associated with another group of Night's children, the *Keres*, daimons who bring humans old age, sickness, death but also beauty and love. The *moira* of each individual is executed by a personal *Ker*. Though sometimes viewed as an external agent, this personal daimon is also viewed as an aspect of one's own character.

Moira, too, can refer to one's own deeds and their inevitable consequences, to what can be attributed to character rather than to some outer cause. Sometimes, of course, like all of us, characters in Greek literature blame an evil daimon for misfortunes they have brought on themselves. In Euripides' *Electra* Orestes learns that he had been wrong to obey Apollo's order to slay his mother, wrong to have thought he had to obey; it was not some divine decree but his own character that determined his *moira*. Not all things are bound; we may make additional trouble for ourselves beyond (though not contrary to) what is allotted to us.[4] Thus Homer has Zeus say, "What blame mortals lay upon the gods! For they say that evils come from us. But they themselves by their own follies have woes beyond what is assigned."[5]

Essentially, then, by destiny the Greeks seem to have meant a recognition of limits to life which we humans are powerless to alter and what we do with the limits that are assigned. Destiny provides the materials and tools with which we shape our lives. A similar analysis of how different acceptance of destiny is from fatalism or determinism is provided in Paul Tillich's essay "Philosophy and Fate": "Where there is no freedom, there is no destiny; there is simply necessity. . . . The more freedom there is, *that is,* the more self-determination, the more susceptibility to destiny." As Tillich goes on to say:

> Destiny signifies that freedom and necessity are not separated but that, in every destiny-full event, freedom and necessity interpenetrate each other. Humans feel that side of their being upon which they have put their own stamp, their "character," is

largely responsible for what happens to them, even external and accidental things. And they feel, at the same time, that their character is conditioned by events that in their origin go far back to past generations, back to much earlier manifestations of the continuing and living fabric of humanity.[6]

For Tillich accepting destiny means accepting our "thrown-ness," our bodies, and our historicity, Coming to terms with destiny means "standing in existence" and acknowledging the inescapable power of the unconscious, prerational levels of the psyche through which destiny determines thought.

How close this is to Freud's understanding. For, although the dictum, anatomy is fate, is often carelessly attributed to him, Freud's translators were actually careful to render his *die Anatomie ist das Schicksal* as "anatomy is destiny." The phrase occurs twice in Freud. First, in the 1912 essay "On the Universal Tendency to Debasement in Love," where Freud brings it into his discussion of how the intimate inseparable conjunction of our excremental and sexual organs serves as a forcible reminder of the inescapably instinctual, animal component of all human love. Freud's thesis here is that the impossibility of adjusting the claims of the sexual drive to the demands of civilization means that renunciation and suffering cannot be avoided by our species.[7] Nothing specific to women appears in this passage,

The other, more often cited instance occurs in the 1924 essay "The Dissolution of the Oedipus Complex," the first essay in which Freud hints at his dawning recognition that female psychology is not simply the mirror image of male psychology. Freud, admitting that the psychoanalytical understanding of female development is still "obscure and full of gaps," introduces the phrase to indicate that he nevertheless assumes that "the morphological distinction {between the sexes} is bound to find expression in differences of psychical development."[8]

Both times Freud uses the phrase, he introduces it as a variation on the phrase "geography is destiny," which Napoleon used to account for his defeat in Russia. Freud is trying to remind us that, just as the imperial invader was forced to acknowledge his limits, we humans must all come to accept the inescapability of material considerations, the ineluctable ways that the body affects the psyche. The same theme appears in *The Future of an Illusion* when Freud invokes *Ananke*, the goddess Necessity, the holder of lots who directs the course of all things. To pay

Ananke the homage due her involves, he claims, coming to terms with the human lot, with limitation and finitude, with mortality.

Reading the discussions within the psychoanalytical community during the 1920s about the psychology of women reveals that though Freud never said "anatomy is fate," others came very close to doing so. Despite significant differences among them, Ernest Jones, Karen Horney, and Helene Deutsch were agreed in saying that women are born not made, that female passivity is a biological given as is female heterosexual desire. At first reading, these theorists may seem to be improving on Freud by critiquing his phallocentrism with their affirmations that women are women—not castrated males, but women. Jones, for example, claims that young girls are feminine and receptive from birth rather than as a result of the failure of their masculinity; femininity develops, he says, as an instinctual unfolding not as a response to the external experience of seeing a penis. Female sexuality is from the beginning focused on the vagina rather than the clitoris, and a woman's deepest anxiety has nothing to do with penis envy but rather reflects her ambivalent fear-of-and-longing-for penetration.[9] Horney claims that there is a primary biological femaleness onto which cultural definitions are imposed; she assumes that there is a feminine nature different from masculinity but of equal value. Unfortunately, she believes, women tend to introject the cultural view of femininity as inferior to masculinity and therefore come to feel an envy of masculinity as well as of the social power it confers.[10] Deutsch, interpreting Freud's description of "normal femininity" as prescriptive rather than as simply a report of a cultural judgment, affirms that the authentically feminine woman will be narcissistic, passive, and masochistic. Females, she believes, experience sexual pleasure not in coitus but in parturition; they find fulfillment by becoming mothers.[11]

Freud, on the other hand, was intrigued by the mystery of how femininity is constructed; he saw that women were not born "feminine" but through the mediation of psychological experience made into what his culture defined as normal femininity:

> I object to all of you to the extent that you do not distinguish more clearly and cleanly between what is psychic and what is biological, that you try to establish a neat parallelism between the two and that you, motivated by such intent, unthinkingly construe psychic facts which are unprovable.[12]

A Poetics of the Body

Although Freud often himself makes use of body imagery, often speaks of penis envy and castration fear, the body is for him really a metaphor for the soul. Much of his discourse relies on synecdoche, the figure of speech in which a part is used to stand for the whole. Freud's usage is genuinely metaphorical. As Naomi Goldenberg discerns:

> The early discovery that memory resides in the body means that in psychoanalysis every physical experience is metaphoric. . . . For psychoanalysis, the flesh can never be literal since, as long as it lives, it teems with past memories and wishes for the future. Body is forever imagining its desires and forever elaborating its past.[13]

Unlike Lacan, Freud does not separate penis, the literal physical member, from phallus, its symbolic meaning. For Freud "penis" signifies both the male genital and what Lacan calls "the Law of the Father." Nor in Freud is the male body the only stimulus to symbolic elaboration. He writes with equal force in accounting for the power of incest longing of how we adults still long for the womb. This is not just simile; a metaphor is always more than "just a metaphor." From Freud's perspective there is no other image that can so fully represent our longing to be fully contained and fully provided for, and no actually available embrace that can fully satisfy that longing.

I, too, believe that we respond to these body parts—to penises, wombs, breasts—symbolically. What interests me is the challenge to do so more consciously, to become more aware of the feelings and images associated with various aspects of our bodies. We might then come to be able to see the anatomical members as figures of our relation to ourselves, to others, and to our surroundings.

It seems that my plan to write a poetics of the psyche has led me almost inevitably now to engage in composing a poetics of the body. The process is almost unavoidably circular and always still incomplete. We are always already imagining our bodies, responding to them through culturally inherited images, and then re-imagining them. A poetics of the body is inescapably a creation or recreation of the body. We have no access to some "real," precultural, before language, before experience, body. Yet how difficult it is not to identify our images with "reality," not to let them harden, how challenging to stay in touch with the polyvalence of bodily experience, to remember we are speaking metaphorically.

As we noted earlier, instead of saying that anatomy is destiny, it might be more accurate to say that destiny is anatomy![14] To a large degree we view our bodies as culture not anatomy itself prescribes. And, of course, as de Beauvoir understood, there are reasons why we sometimes prefer to think anatomy is fate, for that leaves us free of the responsibility for choosing what our bodies mean.

Yet, as I also noted there, it seems to me mistaken to substitute cultural determinism for anatomical fatalism. In the earlier chapter I focused on the social construction of the body; here I want to focus on the body itself, want to find a way of honoring my ambivalence about deconstructionism. For there is a sense in which deconstructionism seems but the latest version of the old human dream of transcending the material, the fleshly, the natural, of asserting once again the superiority of the cultural, social, spiritual. (And, as Jane Gallop notes, the Lacanian substitution of phallus for penis encourages us to see the phallus as disembodied, self-sufficient, spiritual; the emblem of male embodiment becomes a sign of transcendence over the "physical.")[15]

Just as I want to affirm that men, too, and not only women may recognize the importance of acknowledging our embodiment, so I also want to acknowledge that women are not immune to the pull to transcendence. As Goldenberg notes, there is something true to what feels like immediate experience in the separation of soma and psyche, something attractive to all of us in the notion of the transcendence of mind over body.[16] The human attraction to antithetical thinking we considered in an earlier chapter encourages us to separate body from mind—as does our longing not to be mortal. But insistence on the dichotomy as *the* truth about the relation of bodies and souls can become pathological. As Adrienne Rich says, it is time for us to learn to "think through the body," time to see the body as a site of knowledge, rather than as something to get beyond or dominate.[17] In an unforgettable metaphor Jane Gallop remarks that if we think the mind/body split through the body, it becomes an image of shocking violence, a "decapitation."[18]

I believe, even if I can't fully defend the belief philosophically, that something about our embodiment asserts itself against cultural images as always already there and thus keeps reimagining alive, keeps us from being wholly captivated by the regnant images (though, of course, these reassertions themselves emerge as images.) My guess is that it is something close to this conviction that led Freud to his notion of *das Es*, of the unconscious instinctual "that" in us emerging in psychical, that is, image, form and that led Jung to his notion of archetype. We don't inherit psychical images but we do inherit bodies capable of certain experiences which trigger memories and hopes, associations and images— and if we fail to engage such images consciously, they will nonetheless resound in our psyches.

Of course what I am really talking about is my experience of *my* body not of "the body." Adrienne Rich is right. We "need a moratorium on saying 'the body' ":

> To write "my body" plunges me into lived experience, par-
> ticularity. I see scars, disfigurements, discolorations, damages,
> losses, as well as what pleases me. . . . To say "the body" lifts
> me away from what has given me a primary perspective. To say
> "my body" reduces the temptation to grandiose assertions.[19]

I don't really believe this is more true of women than of men. I don't believe we women have an unmediated relation to our bodies such that our sexuality and identity can escape symbolic structuring. I don't believe in a feminine essence that precedes or transcends cultural defi-nition. Both men and women are embodied, both are culturally defined —and both "maleness" and "femaleness" are more polyvalent than our usual images admit. How likely we are, for example, to identify male-ness with the penis, or rather with the phallus, the fantasmal always erect penis, and to ignore the flaccid penis, the vulnerable testicles, the penetrable anus. (To articulate a poetics of the male body is something I will leave to men, though if I were to essay it I might begin with Delmore Schwartz's poem, "The Heavy Bear Who Goes With Me.")

Nonetheless, for reasons that are no doubt in part cultural and in part physiological (for instance, the unavoidable reminder imposed by our monthly bleeding), we women may remember our embodiment more easily, may be more likely consciously to seek to understand and to valorize its significance. In any case, some of us do remember and that, I believe, is profoundly important for all of us, women and men, right now.

I also believe it is important not to restrict our reflecting on and with our bodies to the theme of sexual difference —for, most significantly, I see attending to what our bodies may remind us of as impressing upon us that as embodied humans we are finite and mortal participants in a network of embodied life. Nevertheless, in this chapter my emphasis will fall upon those aspects of bodily experience peculiar to women.

Once again I want to speak from my experience as a woman to other women— with a sense men might be listening in. Once again I imagine us in the center of a clearing performing our sacred rites, knowing that the men of the tribe stand at its edge, as though they belong, but there at the periphery. This time I imagine the ritual taking place in full sunlight, not at night. And, though Artemis may be the presiding deity, I sense Aphrodite as also close by. For we need her encouragement as we dare this exposure of our bodies, as we, like the goddess of beauty and love, show ourselves willing to be seen unclothed.

Again to say to women: I cannot know what of this is also true of you or only of me.

Again I say to men: I cannot say what of this is true of you or only true of us. Only you can know how this is relevant to your understanding of women, to your understanding of yourselves.

Both myths and rituals help us live more deeply, but rituals (which are predicated on the recognition of the importance of bodily participation) are especially relevant here in this context where we seek to acknowledge and celebrate our embodiment. Rituals involve motion and emotion, not only idea and story.

> *The way toward each other is through our bodies.*
> *Words are the longest distance you can travel*
> *so complex and hazardous you*
> *lose your direction.*
> . . . .
> *the possibility of touching.* [20]

Through participation in the ritual we seek to know what our bodies can teach us about our souls. Rites are events; something happens that is transformative not just representative. They remind us that our femaleness is not just a biological given but something that we create together through our activity. Ritual has performative power.

The Mysteries of Female Embodiment

Rituals initiate us into an awareness of being female and of what that signifies. Initiations, beginning as acts of separation, as the death of a prior self, always involve a loss of innocence. Typically they proceed through a descent into a kind of underworld: Demeter loses a daughter; Persephone loses her virginity; Hera loses her trust in Zeus's fidelity; Artemis loses her dream of an unthreatened autonomy; Aphrodite suffers the loss of her beloved. Rituals that initiate us into our femininity force us to leave behind the innocence that precedes gender differentiation.

Rituals involve action, gesture, touch. To imagine this exploration of our female embodiment as a ritual means to imagine touching our breasts, our vulva, our clitoris, means remembering how they feel from inside. The possibility of touching initiates us into a different kind of knowing of our bodies and of one another than we can achieve through seeing, through looking at, into an apprehension of our bodies not as the site of medical problems (which male doctors might know how to treat) but as a place of mystery, as a place of encounter with the sacred.

We attend to them as to the sacred. We approach them like a text to be read, like a dream which cannot be entirely de-ciphered. Jane Gallop speaks of "an eternal reading of the 'body' as an authorless text, full of tempting, persuasive significance, but lacking a final guarantee of intended meaning"— like, I would add, what Freud called the "navel" of dream, that in the dream which resists interpretation, which leads deep down to the unfathomable, unverbalizable unconscious. Gallop speaks of our bodies as a series of "perceptible givens that the human being knows as 'hers' without knowing their significance to her."[21]

The aim in attending to our bodies, as in attending to dreams, is to establish a more conscious relationship to them. We have female bodies: what does that mean to us? We vary enormously not only in how we live having periods, having clitorises and vaginas, wombs and breasts, but also in the importance we attach to these aspects of our being. For some they may seem almost irrelevant, to others central; to some simply a matter of biology that they have to come to terms with, for others of deep symbolic import. I would also bid us to remember that there is no such thing as "the" female body. Each body is different; each is us, fits us. Kim Chernin agrees: "Shall I say we are all, each one of us, in a body we've chosen? The body that matches up with us. Everything else is a lie, daydream, mere ambition. What we are, need to be, is that body."[22]

Nonetheless, I believe attending to the particularities of my experience of my female body initiates me into apprehensions which I share with many other women and which are also available to men (if they are encouraged to imagine their own bodies and even perhaps women's!), but not as easily.

I am interested not simply in what it means to have a female body but in what it means to have periods, breasts, a vagina. I want to encourage us to attend to each of these particular aspects of our embodiment, to be open to the many images each evokes, the many and often contradictory feelings each inspires. I am persuaded that our relation to each part of our body will inevitably be informed by our particular life story, but I also believe it need not be fully determined by that history. We are capable of imagining perspectives other than those our own experience has taught us, capable of moving toward richer, more subtly and complexly nuanced relationships. To give each part of our body its due is to adopt a polytheistic understanding of our embodiment. Each part represents a world of meanings, just as each goddess or god in the pantheon represents a particular mode of apprehension, a particular world. Yet somehow we want also to remember that we are not just breasts *and* vaginas *and* wombs, want also to remain aware of the whole in which each participates.

Like Alma Luz Villanueva I want to sing of the female body:

> (wo)man
>   Yes Woman!
> I celebrate our bodies,
> our wombs, intact and perfect even as we're born
> out of our mother's
>   womb
> I celebrate
> because most
> men have forgotten
> how to . . .
>
> I rejoice in the slick/red walls of our
>   wombs,

the milk of our breasts
the ecstasy of our clitoris
and our need of man when we
open our legs and womb
to him
      the bloody circle thru our daughters
      and sons

I want to fly and sing
of our beauty and power.
to re/awaken this joy
in us all;
      our power lies in being Woman[23]

   In my own "singing" I want to reflect on what it means to have bodies like those of our mothers, what it means to menstruate and then stop, what it means to us to have a clitoris and a vagina, wombs, breasts, bodies that age and die. Reclaiming our bodies means also reclaiming the language we use when we speak of them —avoiding as much as we can the technical Latinate words, uterus, ovaries, parturition, lactation—speaking instead of wombs and eggs, bleeding and birth. I want to share my reflections on how our experience of these different aspects of our female embodiment shapes us, shapes our hopes and fears, our sense of what life offers and withholds—but also how each provides metaphors for experiences in other realms of our life. I hope to help us imaginatively enter into ways of experiencing these various parts of our own body that our particular history may not have included, so that our consciousness of what each can mean may be expanded.

Women Born of Woman

I begin by reflecting on what it might mean to us that our bodies are like those of our mothers, our source, for I sense that may contribute to our awareness of the sacredness of our own bodies which have the same birth-giving, creative power as theirs.
   I don't know how early we know this or just what it is that we know. I know that I had almost no conscious information about conception or birth until long after I first went to school. Yet I also know that in the

earliest dream I can remember (a dream I dreamt often in my childhood but which I know I first dreamt while we were still in Germany, before I turned four), I make my way through a narrow dark passageway to a room lined with crimson velvet drapes and carpeted in red. At its center is a jewel-studded treasure chest. It is the most peaceful and beautiful space I have ever entered. Only I have keys to the room or to the chest. Only I have ever seen either. And though I go there rarely, the room is always available to me. From the vantage point of my adult acquaintance with Freud and Jung it seems to me undeniable that this red room represents both womb and self. Is the womb my mother's or mine? Must it not be both?

I have written in an earlier chapter of my reservations about the emphasis some feminist object-relations theorists have laid upon the developmental impact of our having an original bond with another like ourselves. They claim that the early experience of being a separate person and yet not radically different from their primary caregiver makes women more empathic and less fearful of intimacy than men. For many of us this may ring true but I'm still not sure how literally or universally to understand it. I do think many mothers feel a particular kind of closeness to their female daughters, though I imagine it as often intertwined with premature grieving on their behalf, or with competition and envy, or resentment. I imagine that mothers communicate their sense of identification with their infant children in many indirect ways, in how they hold them, in what behaviors they encourage or discourage, in what of their own feelings they share with them. And I imagine that as daughters we do pick up on this, though I also suspect some of us may from early on reject the projection—and, nonetheless, may also from early on feel we cannot entirely escape it.

That first fusionlike closeness may, indeed, color our lifelong sense of what intimate relationships "should" be like, may induce an unappeasable nostalgia for an irrecoverable intimacy. But I suspect that this vision of closeness is more retrospective fantasy than objective memory, that it is more about what Jung would call the archetypal mother than about our actual mothers and that in reality many of us, as Adrienne Rich so well expressed it, feel "wildly unmothered." We feel we were devoured by our mothers, abandoned by them, or abducted from them. Indeed, we may feel all of this. We may come to feel profound ambivalence toward our mother and to feel that our relation to our father is less problematic. Just because our mothers are there from the beginning, it seems incredibly difficult for many of us to keep the archetype and the woman whom Jung calls "its accidental carrier" distinct. We make the separation—and then find ourselves having to do so all over again.

I believe that the image of being like our mothers is to many of us a terrifying specter. We are afraid of being like them. We cry out, Must my life be like hers? In the next chapter I reflect on how in my own later years this question, which I had thought to have dealt with long ago, has returned to haunt me.

I have also become more and more aware of the *particular* ways in which my body is like my mother's. It is not just that we both have wombs and breasts, but that my gestures, my facial expressions, the rhythms of my speech, my posture are hers. She lives in me, in precisely those aspects of my being which feel most intimately, most concretely *me*. It feels as though I cannot escape her presence.

The likeness between mothers and daughters is a source of blessing, as it connects us to the sacrality of our own body—and a curse. For it seems enormously difficult to step out of that mother-daughter bond— to move beyond staying at some central point in our psyche, daughter. Still full of expectation that another will fully meet our needs. Still full of resentment that no one does.

The object-relations theorists write of how the achievement of autonomy, independence, self-sufficiency may be more difficult for women. But maybe, *maybe*, it is also easier for us to recognize that both dependence and independence are illusions and thus to move to that recognition of human interdependence which almost every psychological theory seems to recognize as *the* sign of maturity. However, achievement of such maturity requires that we move from being the daughters of our mothers to acknowledging a shared sisterhood with them. We need to move beyond seeing mother as other, as existing only in relation to us, as not having her own desire and rage, her own point of view. It is strange how some of us who passionately protest against having our own female identity defined in terms of our reproductive capacity may nonetheless still see our mothers in ways that revive the identification between femininity and maternity.[24] Perhaps, as in adulthood we experience our own lacks (or potential lacks) as mothers, we can forgive our mothers for theirs, and see how being women, being mothers, means being powerful and vulnerable, giving and needy, wise and foolish. We move from seeing ourselves as like them to recognizing that *they* are like *us*! We are initiated into an understanding of the sacred as encompassing vulnerability and finitude.

Bleeding and Ceasing to Bleed

If there is *an* event that marks our initiation into female embodiment, it may be that beginning at puberty we bleed every month. In many cultures this biological event is given cultural recognition, although, since the transition from childhood into gendered adulthood is so clearly marked on their bodies, females are usually not required to undertake as challenging a puberty ordeal as males. Nevertheless, they are at this point often formally welcomed into the sisterhood of women through a ceremony which celebrates the sacredness of this blood.

Indeed, many of the transformation rituals of women are blood mysteries—mysteries which valorize female blood as synonymous with power over life and death. This bleeding that does not issue from a wound, that signifies creative capacity not injury, evokes wonder, hope, and anxiety. In Hindu culture the sacrality of menstrual and birth blood is suggested by one of the names of the Goddess: She-Who-Bleeds-But-Does-Not-Die. Because menstrual blood is seen as magically potent, it is often closely associated with healing, purification, creative energy. It is used in rituals designed to assure success in the planting or hunting upon which a community's life depends. Menstrual and lunar cycles are the basis of most early calendars.[25] Judy Grahn asserts that, indeed, all rites are menstrual, in that they are periodical. "It is the periodicity of menstruation," she says, "that has made it so important to human affairs."[26]

In many cultures there are elaborate taboos associated with menstrual blood. Although interpreters of these taboos and of the isolation often imposed on menstruating women have traditionally tended to focus on male disgust and fear, recent studies of tribal cultures emphasize the many different meanings and creative possibilities of menstrual taboos, and thus support Harding's contention that women may originally have chosen the periodic withdrawal from social responsibilities in an all-female enclave.[27] I have been intrigued and moved by how in my own experience, when I have shared a household with several women, we have soon all come to have our periods at the same time; it may well be that in small-scale tribal cultures all the women of the community menstruated at once. In some cultures women flauntingly announce that they are menstruating by wearing special clothes or jewelry. Grahn suggests that the way in which at puberty some girls in our culture begin wearing lipstick may represent a faint echo of such ancient practices.[28] I remember Carol Christ once sharing with me a fantasy of going out into the world when she was having her period wearing white slacks and no pad, no tampon, and thus proudly announcing, "I'm a menstruating woman."

In a female ritual context menstruation means more than the beginning of reproductive capacity; it means initiation into shared sisterhood with all who bleed. I know women who have sought to create menstrual rituals together. They save their blood and pour it onto the earth. They break the taboo against this blood by doing this not alone but in each other's company. They tell each other their stories of first bleeding. They welcome one another into the circle of women, knowing many were not welcomed when that blood first flowed. They tell one another the stories of the humiliation of the blood. The ugly names. The words of disgust. The acts of withdrawal. They tell one another of the gifts of being woman, of the moments of pleasure being female has given them. They give themselves new names. They find new names for their bleeding. They create rituals to reimagine their own initiation into womanhood. They create these rituals to provide a re-initiation for themselves and a different kind of initiation for their daughters.[29]

Although one's first menstrual period is a distinct event, the transition does not really happen all at once. It is preceded by years of anticipation. Long before we begin to bleed, our understanding of what it means is shaped by what we are told and not told, by the feelings about it communicated to us directly or indirectly by our mothers and grandmothers, our older sisters, our peers. We may look forward expectantly or with dread. We may note with tender regard or with muted anxiety the first faint swellings on our once-flat chests, the first prickly pubic hairs. We may also discover that what it means to us to be menstruating women keeps unfolding and expanding throughout our lives. It didn't all happen then, at the beginning.

Nevertheless, for many of us our first period represents a fateful, never forgotten moment. Many women of my generation still harbor anger about how their mothers responded to their first bleeding. Mine had done nothing to prepare me. Had it not been for the somewhat confused whisperings among my friends, I might have been terrified as I first found blood on the toilet paper. I still recall how when I came down to the kitchen to tell my mother, to ask her what to do, she handed me a pad and a belt and, all without looking, told me to be sure to wrap the soiled pads well and then immediately put them in the kitchen garbage so my father and brother might never have to be troubled by them. When she tried to say something about what this bleeding signified, it was so evident that she didn't know what to say or how, that in pity I hastened to tell her I already knew all about it. Though I knew I didn't. Yet I did somehow know that I was determined to protect myself from her view of menstruation as a kind of "curse," her acceptance of the male view of it as a "pollution."

How I envied Sharon Olds when I read her poem "The Moment":

> When I saw the dark Egyptian stain,
> I went down into the house to find you, Mother . . .
> You looked up from the iron sink,
> a small haggard pretty woman
> of 40, one week divorced.
> "I've got my period, Mom," I said,
> and saw your face abruptly break open and
> glow with joy. "baby," you said,
> coming toward me, hands out and
>   covered with tiny delicate bubbles like seeds.[30]

I understood later how much my mother had suffered from premenstrual headaches and from menstrual cramps, how she couldn't possibly rejoice for me. I know that this is not just a matter of her being a woman of a generation different from my own. Some women of my age (and, no doubt, of my daughter's too) share the feelings my mother silently communicated and to which Marge Piercy (a contemporary of mine not hers) gives voice in her poem "Something to Look Forward To":

> My friend Penny at twelve being handed a napkin
> the size of an ironing board cover, cried out
> Do I have to do this from now until I die?
> No, said her mother, it stops in middle age.
> Good, said Penny, there's something to look forward to.
>
> Today supine, groaning with demon crab claws
> gouging my belly, I tell you I will secretly dance

and pour out a cup of wine on the earth
when time stops that leak permanently;
I will burn my last tampons as votive candles.[31]

But I remember with joy a winter afternoon when I and a woman friend were lying on my bed listening to music, while her husband and mine sat downstairs watching football on TV. There was a gentle knock on the door and then my daughter's voice asking if she might come in. "Can I come lie with you, too?" she asked. "I've just become a woman." So she came and lay between us, half as a child might lie between her parents, half as another woman there among us. When the slow, lovely music ended, she said, "I'd like to do something to celebrate." "What?" we asked. "I don't quite know," she began. And then more certainly, "I'd like us to make a feast for the whole family, a vegetable stew and some fresh baked bread." So we three went to the store and found what we needed and spent the rest of the afternoon in the kitchen. When it came time to eat, my daughter proudly told her brothers and her father what we were celebrating. And her brothers to my great delight knew that this was an occasion for celebration not teasing. (I hadn't been sure they would know.)

The relation to menstruation seems to serve as a real touchstone of the differences among women. Feminists seem drawn either to glorify or to trivialize this aspect of female life. It can mean so many different things, can serve as a source of pride or shame, can be experienced as an embarrassing secret or as an annoying nuisance. Some of us almost ignore this monthly emission, as I did in my youth, proud that I never felt any physical discomfort or emotional dislocation, never experienced any disruption of my usual routines. Others among us may be devastated, some months or every month, just before we bleed or as we bleed, by emotional tension or physical pain. Some of us are perturbed by such signs of "female weakness," and believe such distress should be "fixed" by resort to some form of psychological or medical therapy. Others see in premenstrual tension not pathology but a form (often preconscious) of social protest, a natural rebellion against the antihuman constraints of modern capitalist life which, they hope, might (as we become more conscious of our dis-ease) be rechanneled into more direct and effective expressions of anger.[32]

Having periods can mean so many different things, but so can not having them. Being the first or the last in a group of peers to get one's period is something we seem to remember all our lives. I am aware of how to this day I still feel a special bond with late bloomers like myself. I know how women who don't have regular periods may experience this as a painful deficiency which cuts them off from full participation in the sisterhood of women.

There are so many images floating around of what menstruation can mean, should mean, does mean, that it is often difficult to be clear what it means to *me*. I have sought to learn how to listen to my body and to try to tune out the ideas I have about it. This can be difficult. I have discovered how tempted I remain too quickly to turn body to image, into a soul event which leaves the actual body experience behind. I have been immeasurably helped in my own listening-to by the testimony of other women, particularly that of my ritual-making friend, Merida Wexler. Robert Musil once wrote, "We do not have too much intellect and too little soul, but too little precision in matters of the soul."[33] I would paraphrase this to say, "We do not have too much intellect and too little body, but too little precision in matters of the body." And it is for such precision about her own emotional and physical experience that I thank Merida. I see her as teaching me "to honor what is generally defiled, to raise to consciousness what has been repressed,"[34] to remember that (though the dominant culture may do much to encourage us to stifle and deny this aspect of our lives) our bleeding is a gift not to be despised or rejected. From a series of letters written to me over the course of several years I have culled these reflections:

> I write today as I bleed. The first day and heaviest flow. I write feeling my weightedness, the drag of my uterus. Feeling my wound, my incapacity. All the changes in my body—my voice flattened, my belly swollen, my clumsiness, a flood of dreams I cannot bring back to consciousness.
>
> How difficult it is to stay in the body. I get up, get to the bathroom, reach into my vagina for the menstrual sponge—a bloody mess! Squeeze the blood into a cup. It splatters everywhere.
>
> Can I write this to you? Am I so crazy I don't even know it? Today I feel such self-doubt.
>
> The knowledge of taboo returns. The blood is not to be touched, let alone saved.
>
> Even what we value of menstruation—are our bodies there? We value the rhythmic cycle, the feelings, the dreams, the bond.

We talk and interpret. Analyze dreams. Theorize. Baroque
elaborations. Virginal fluffy clouds. Ascending out of the blood,
the mess, the ache, the wound.

Even this writing. How difficult for me to stay with my body.
My feelings of vulnerability. My tears that I had hoped were past,
falling again. Fears and doubts.

Here I am. My weight, my slowness, my softness, my
thoughts drifting by, my dulling to the exterior setting, turning
inward.

Here I am. The ache in my lower spine is sensual, as is the
openness of my vulva, my blood slipping in my vagina.

A wound not to be healed — but attended to—felt,
touched, smelled, seen. Received.[35]

Merida's words remind me of how our monthly periods open us to
our vulnerability, our tears, our doubts, our fears, to a sense of wounds
as not to be fixed but attended to. She encourages us to honor our
dreams, the dreams we have that prepare us for our bleeding, the
dreams that accompany our bleeding, the dreams that warn us we may
cease to bleed.

In a similar vein Kathee Miller's poem "Mysteries," describes how our
monthly bleeding initiates us into a kind of order different from that
associated with the linear, goal-directed orientation that mostly holds us
(and not only men) in its sway. The rhythms of our body encourage us
to honor the rhythms of our souls, our need for times of extroversion
and times of introversion. This attunement to our bodies may help us
remember how ineluctably we are part of nature and related to its cyclic,
repetitive rhythms, the rhythms of tide and moon.

> Women bleed each month invisible
> what could be life sheds itself
> in rhythms and tides of the moon
> invisibly we ache and bleed and feel
> open in our blood strength
> some feel ugly some beautiful. . .
> sometimes we bleed down our legs in the shower
> or into the sea upon grassy meadows
> the earth receives our blood rites[36]

Having periods may mean different things to us at different times in
our life. Initially it may mean joining fully a group of peer maidens, of

feeling a closeness to other females going through the same physical and emotional changes. It may then lead to an urge to explore our sexuality, often particularly our heterosexuality. Later we may look forward to the approach of our periods with hope or fear, fear of being pregnant, fear of not being pregnant. Later still we may wonder each month, is this the last time I will bleed? What will it be like not to bleed? If we have come to depend on this monthly reminder to keep us in touch with our inner rhythms, we may, like Merida, wonder: "What happens when it ends? What do I listen to inside? What do I move to? I imagine a more subtle hearing is necessary."[37]

And there may come a time when it is another's bleeding that keeps us in touch with all that menstruation means. I think that I was more aware of how our periods shape our lives into a cyclic rhythm after menopause than I ever had been before. The woman I live with is sixteen years younger than I, and for several years we hoped she might have a child. To rely on artificial insemination for conception makes it a very conscious and tension-filled process, indeed. How much our lives during those years were shaped by our constant attunement to River's monthly cycle—to our own seasons of preparation, attempt, hope, disappointment, and the renewal of hope.

After years of having our lives defined by this monthly bleeding, at menopause we cease to bleed. In the years since I wrote my book on menopause I have become even more aware how varied are women's responses to this transition, how for some this, too, is a taboo and secret shame, and for others a welcome opportunity to explore what they are now ready to leave behind and what is now newly available. We may discover that unconsciously we feel differently than consciously, that the change represents more of a loss than expected. Some of us who have resented the patriarchal view that identifies femininity with maternity discover to our surprise that we no longer feel fully female when no longer defined by our reproductive capacity. For some this is a time of gain; for others, of painful loss; for most of us, probably both.

I've also become more aware of how much my own exploration took for granted the "naturalness" of the event, took for granted its occurring in my early fifties, took for granted that I wouldn't suffer exhausting hot flashes or the vaginal dryness that for some makes intercourse so painful it becomes almost impossible. I didn't realize the degree to which my feelings about menopause were shaped by my being a healthy and successful middle-class professional woman who had borne and raised children. Nor did I fully realize how entrenched the view of menopause as a pathology still is.

Because I had chosen not to take estrogen, I had given little thought to how strangely menopause may be experienced by those who choose hormonal therapy and may find themselves in an odd no-woman's land, postmenopausal in one sense and yet still having periods nonetheless.

Because I went through menopause just about when I'd always assumed I would, I gave little thought to how differently the cessation of bleeding might be experienced when it comes "prematurely." Forced passages, passages which we are required to navigate "out of turn," often feel like the intrusion of the "unnatural" into the natural. The too-soonness of a medical hysterectomy may feel like yet another abduction, another experience of being taken from oneself too abruptly, too quickly. Though recognizing that the operation may be a lifesaver, we may yet be overwhelmed by the sense of not knowing enough to know for certain that that is so, by the feeling of being out of control, dependent on a male doctor who may have no sense of the inner cost of the loss. We may find ourselves precipitated into a stage of life for which we are not ready. And may discover there are so few helpers, so little permission to rage and mourn.

Again my friend Merida, who had been consciously preparing for menopause and then suddenly found herself precipitated into it, has helped me to understand what this must be like:

> All I've written about soul and spirit in the body is now being tested by this event.
>
> My grief. This is how menopause comes to me. This my menopause journey. A single gate. The ground opening beneath me even as narcissus, crocus and now purple hyacinth open to bloom in my backyard garden.
>
> A single swift abduction. No return. I feel maiden-taken inexorably.
>
> In the underworld again. And maiden Persephone. I thought her remote, but she is vividly here. And mother as well. A doubling.
>
> An enraged grieving mother above. Active. Watchful. Furious. The daughter below. Stunned in pain.[38]

I have also learned much from the women who have participated in the workshops on menopause I've led since the publication of my book. I was surprised by the wide age range of the women who came to these groups. Some were women in their seventies, who felt that though they had gone through the physical transition years ago, they had not yet fully understood its soul meaning. There were also women in their early thirties who came because of a felt need to begin to get ready for changes that still lay far ahead. One group of five such women came together. They had known each other since nursery school, supported one another through their first periods and first sexual experiences, their marriages, births, miscarriages, and divorces—and now wanted to prepare together for the next major change they were likely to face.

In these workshops we talked together about the images and feelings we have about menstruation and reproduction, about what we knew and didn't know about the physical and emotional changes usually associated with menopause, about our hopes and fears. We talked about our guides, male and female, about fellow travelers, about hindrances and hinderers. We told one another our life stories and our dreams. We collaborated in the creation of a ritual.

We talked about what rituals accomplish, how they provide validation of the importance of a life passage and give us symbols through which we can express the ambivalence its approach stirs up in us. Rituals provide a way of sharing which honors both the personal and the communal aspects of an experience; they free us from living it in isolation without flattening the experience to some lowest common denominator. A ritual allows us to complete something, and then to return to our familiar lives, knowing that in some important ways we are different than we were before participation in the rite.

We knew we would have to create our own ritual, that there were no models. We began with an *invocation*. Each of us chose a particular figure whom we wanted to thank for helping us move toward or through this transition, or one whose support we wanted to invite, or one with whom we needed to be reconciled before we could possibly go on. Some of us chose an older woman who might serve as our guide; some of us chose a peer friend who might be a companion; some of us addressed our invocation to a goddess.

We then each offered up a *sacrifice* of something that needed to be given up so that we might make the transition. For some it was something already yielded; for others, something we wished we'd had the courage to leave behind but hadn't yet been able to; for others, something we still half-hoped might be spared. Whatever it was, we found something concrete to represent it and then literally buried the object in the earth. Naming it and naming our regrets. Mourning the loss.

We then sought to name what we imagined as the *boon* that living this transition consciously, hopefully, might grant us. We offered our pleas. We offered our thanks.

We concluded with a *benediction*. We formed two lines, facing each other. In one stood all the women who felt themselves still in the preparation phase; in the other, all those who felt they had already made the transition. (Those somewhere in its midst had to choose which felt more true of them at least for the hour of the ceremony.) One by one the women in the younger group said whatever they had to say to those in the other, were they words of gratitude or blame or imploration. And one by one the women in the other group addressed those across the room with their words, were they words of encouragement or regret or warning.

And at the ritual's end, all of us in chorus chanted, "May we all learn to honor the pains and joys of this passage. May we learn to honor those who go before us, to support those who follow."

Sexual Awakening and Fulfillment

The loss of virginity is yet another female blood mystery which we may be reluctant to celebrate, though for very different reasons. Because it implies that our discovery of our own capacity for sensual pleasure is dependent on men, there is something about the view of first intercourse as the awakening of female sexuality which may strike us as a male fantasy. The emphasis on virginity and first intercourse seems to separate out coital penetration as *the* sexual act and to denigrate all noncoital sexuality as infantile or perverse. Like some contemporary feminists Freud related the fetishization of virginity to a male fantasy of having control over the female body and, at a deeper level, to male fear and envy of female generativity.[39]

But, as we noted in the first chapter, "virginity," need not be understood primarily in physical terms, as referring to an intact hymen; it may instead, as Harding suggests, signify a woman's in-her-selfness. We may recall that there is no account of Aphrodite, the goddess most closely associated with physical love, being initiated into her sexuality. Always already in touch with her own sexuality, she never loses her virginity.

Guilia Sassa says that the Greeks explicitly denied the very facticity of the "so-called virginal membrane" which we tend to fetishize; they understood "virginity" to apply not to a particular part of a woman's body but to her whole being. Sassa explores the complex intercorrelation of secrecy, silence, and virginity: what a father or bridegroom doesn't know, in a legal and social sense, hasn't happened. Unsuspected sexual experience does not entail the loss of virginal status; the experience is completely the maiden's own; she is still a virgin.[40] And as countless myths testify, the Greeks saw virginity was something that could be lost and *regained.*[41]

In E. M. Broner's wonderful novel *A Weave of Women*, a circle of Israeli women gather soon after one of them has given birth to a daughter and perform a ritual "hymenectomy," modeled after the Jewish rite of male circumcision. The women gently pierce the baby's hymen and then each in turn tells the story of her own defloration, some humiliating, some triumphant. Through performance of the ritual they hope to endow the child with an Aphrodite-like access to her sexuality as her own.[42]

When coitus is identified as *the* sex act, it seems to follow that female sexual fulfillment *should* be found there. We don't always recognize the degree to which the emphasis on intercourse, orgasm, and heterosexuality represents a male model of sexuality, perhaps partly because many of us have been initiated into orgasmic sexuality by men, sometimes by gentle, sensitive men who seemed to know our bodies better than we knew them ourselves. Because it can be a powerful experience to be brought in touch with the intensity of our own desire for the first time, as it can also be stunning to discover our power to evoke and fulfill desire in another, we may forget that earlier experiences of touching ourselves with pleasure, of cuddling with girl friends, of fantasizing ecstatic encounters with imagined lovers, were also sexual experiences.

My own first experience of intercourse has long since almost faded from memory; it was really a hardly noticeable event in a continuum of events from heavy petting to an ability to fully enjoy, initiate, experiment sexually. But I vividly remember a fantasy of first intercourse, a fantasy that accompanied lovemaking with a familiar and beloved partner, a fantasy which took hold of both of us though neither of us felt we were creating it. As we made love that long, lazy afternoon, it seemed to both of us that we were First Man and First Woman engaged in a delightful and also momentously important discovery. This was not my or our first intercourse, but *the* first intercourse. And still today when I think of sexual awakening, I think of that event which occurred when I was in my early forties, not of the one more than twenty years earlier.

It may, indeed, be true that for some of us another's desire first awakens us to our own; the honest history of our own sexuality may not be entirely congruent with our latter-day politics. But once awakened to our own active desire, how quickly we learn the untruth in the old equation of activity with maleness, passivity with femaleness. There is so much in my sexuality that is not receptive, not primarily responsive, but active, initiative taking, hungry. In fact, there is much evidence to suggest that men have always known that and feared it, that the image of female passivity is counterphobic, apotropaic. As, indeed, the intensity of our desire, its rawness, its wildness, may also sometimes frighten us.

I stand in awe of the sense of shameless delight and pride in her own sexuality communicated by the Sumerian goddess Inanna. As she waits for her lover, she sings:

> My vulva, the horn
> The Boat of Heaven,
> Is full of eagerness like the young moon,
> My untilled land lies fallow.

> As for me, Inanna,
> Who will plow my vulva?
> Who will plow my high field?
> Who will plow my high ground?

Later she describes her pleasure in their lovemaking:

> He stroked my pubic hair,
> He watered my womb.
> He laid his hand on my holy vulva,
> He smoothed my black boat with cream,
> He quickened my narrow boat with milk.
> He caressed me on the bed. [43]

But not all of us have so immediate an access to our bodies. "The body's voice may be so slow, shy, hesitant, deeply withdrawn. . . . How to reach it, read it?"[44] How do we discover the particularities of our own desire and pleasure? How can we learn to stay in touch with body knowledge and memory, to listen consciously to our body's wants? How do we learn to tell the truth about that to ourselves, much less a partner?

My sense is that discovering our own sexuality requires listening not only to our bodies but to our dreams and fantasies. And these may reveal a sexuality frightening in its polyvalence and its voracity, its inclusion of rage and violence. Many of us have nightmares of rape. Many of us dream of tabooed sex, sex with animals, with parents, with children—the kind of sexuality that permeates myths.

It seems important to avoid pretending that all of our bodies are the same, that all of us have the same desire, experience pleasure in the same way—or to lock ourselves into only one desire, one form of pleasure. It seems important that we learn to talk to each other about our sexualities, without shame and without norms. To talk together about "erogenous zones," about clitorises, vaginas, breasts. To seek to speak honestly about our pleasure. To open ourself to the full range of meanings associated with each mode of desire, each site of pleasure. To try to avoid politicizing this conversation prematurely.

When women begin to talk to one another (or to read what other women have written), we quickly discover how little consensus there is among us as to what constitutes the most authentic and fulfilling mode of female sexuality. Some of us point to heterosexual intercourse, others to masturbation, and others to lesbian sex. As we begin to talk about where in our bodies we feel our sexuality to be centered, some among us say the clitoris, others the vagina, still others speak of a suffusion of the whole body which belies the notion of erogenous zones. Can we attend to each of these responses as though each embodies a truth not just about physical pleasure but about how we as humans are related to ourselves, to other women, to men, to the natural world?

Some women claim that masturbation, self-pleasuring, provides the best clue to our "real" sexuality. Shere Hite, for example, seems to assume that through exploration of her own body a woman can learn all the secrets of her own sexuality.[45] And, indeed, our experiences of autoerotic sex may give us access to a "virginal" sexuality, to an awareness of our body's capacity for physical pleasure as an end in itself. While masturbating I am freed from dependence on another for my own fulfillment and freed from attending to another's need and desire rather than my own. I may feel free to focus on sexual fulfillment as a *body* event which transports me out of the world of social constraint; I may feel deeply in touch with my own *nature*.

Yet other women, Jane Gallop, for example, find something oddly "masculine" about Hite's unquestioned emphasis on genitality and "good" orgasms, and her hope of "banishing all mystery which might stand in the way of a woman's self-determination and control over her own body."[46] I understand the critique, yet want to rejoin: masturbatory sex need not focus on orgasms; it may entail a slow, gentle exploration of just what kind of touching my particular body finds most pleasurable at this moment; it may signify an encounter precisely with the mysteriousness and elusiveness of my own sexuality. Yet I, too, am uncomfortable with the view that masturbation provides us with *the* paradigm of true female sexuality, for the understanding of sexuality as *mine* ignores the ways in which so much of what is most important to me about sexuality is what happens *with* and *between*.

The traditions associated with Sappho and with the Artemis temple at Brauron suggest that in classical Greece there were places where girls of marriageable age were taught about their body's capacity for desire and pleasure by other women. Although these young maidens were not being initiated into lifelong lesbianism but rather prepared for heterosexual marriage, the assumption seems to have been that females learn about their sexuality best from other women. The priestesses could teach these younger women about their sexuality, so that even if a husband didn't care about his wife's sexual fulfillment, she would already know how to access it.

In the contemporary world many women see lovemaking among women as providing the best clue to authentic feminine sexuality, as the truly "normal" female sexuality. Some see lesbianism as representing essentially different erotic values and practices from those associated with heterosexuality or male homosexuality. Starting from a feminist political perspective, they condemn as deviant any sexual pleasure that does not serve to enhance female identity. All genuine lesbian sexuality is viewed as mutually consensual, all role playing (such as "butch" and "femme") as oppressive. What matters most is the standard of egalitarian caring relationships: "Pleasure is put in its place, reinforcing sistergood" as an ultimate value.[47] This view seems to imply a sameness among women, a sameness of anatomy, power, and desire, a presumption that "another woman would know instinctively just how to touch me."[48]

I find this affirmation of women's bonds with one another powerful and beautiful—and yet I wonder about the implicit essentialism, the assumption that all women are alike. I sense here an attempt to make our desire consistent with our politics and fear that we may once again be putting ideas ahead of the body. I know women who are deeply committed to women, articulate and passionate feminists, wonderfully dedicated and sensitive friends to the women they love, who have experienced lovemaking with women but found to their regret and sometimes shame that they prefer men as sexual partners. I know women sexually drawn to other women who have nonetheless discovered with real dismay how difficult it is to discover just how their partners most want to be touched, or to communicate to those partners how they themselves most urgently desire to be touched.

Other celebrators of lesbian sexuality acknowledge the differences among women and recognize the subtle, challenging task of learning to read another woman's desire as part of the joy of lesbian interaction. They see the uniqueness of each woman's way of experiencing body pleasure as more likely to be understood by another woman, and assert that what's wrong with heterosexism is that it seeks to impose *a* sexuality on all of us. This lesbianism accepts that some of us may enjoy lovemaking with women *and* with men, and suggests that political lesbianism (with its fetishistic valorization of one mode of sexual expression) is yet another phallicism! The primary metaphor of this lesbianism is the game, the validation of a consciously playful sexuality, a sexuality which is self-reflectively "post-lesbian, post-dyke, post-gay, post-homosexual, avowedly post-postmodernist," which "embraces and transcends every contradiction."[49]

Others see lesbian sexuality not as a superior form of sexuality or as an all-embracing sexuality but rather as a kind of retreat from sexuality, as a return to a presexual sensuality in place of sex. To Stendhal lesbianism represents a

> place where we can heal our wounds from being women, protect each other as women protect their children from the world. From too much adventure, challenge, inequity, competition. In short, from life. . . . Shielding ourselves from the conventional notions of sex (domination, passive surrender, giving up self), we come close to eliminating sex altogether."[50]

Grover agrees, some forms of lesbian sexuality seem "so soft, so uncon-
flicted, so much of a sameness" that the "sex" "might as well be taking
place in the pre-Oedipal world of the nursery."[51]

We women disagree not only about with whom we are most likely
to experience sexual fulfillment but also about where in our bodies that
fulfillment is most intensely felt. In recent decades feminist theorists and
sexologists have often talked about clitoral orgasms as though they
were the only real orgasms a real woman could own up to. And it is true
that many of us experience the most intense physical pleasure through
clitoral stimulation and that many of us don't receive enough of this
stimulation in intercourse. It is also true that many of us first discovered
our own capacity for orgasmic pleasure through clitoral self-pleasuring.

I know this was true of me. I can remember in very early childhood
and again in early adolescence, when I still had no conceptual knowledge of clitorises or vaginas or intercourse or orgasm, delighting in the
pleasurable sensation of rubbing this hidden little button and experiencing its engorgement and detumescence—a wonderful secret pleasure that I never talked about to anyone, that I wasn't sure anyone else
had discovered. I had no sense at all it had anything to do with what
men and women did with one another when they "had sex" or "made
babies." So, yes, in a sense this was *my* sexuality.

But I would not now want to identify my sexuality with clitoral
orgasm or with masturbation. In trying to get beyond the politics of this
discussion, I have sought to discover what is true to my own felt
experience. What I find is that in lovemaking I'm not aware of a focus
on this one place of sensation. Even while masturbating I now always
feel drawn to entering deeply into my vagina with my fingers while the
heel of my hand rubs my clitoris. I stopped using a vibrator long ago
because I didn't like the sharp intensity of the orgasms it brought me,
which felt too localized and left me in some ways more tense than when
I'd begun.

Some castigate Freud for ignoring clitoral sexuality, while others
recognizing (as did he) the homology between clitoris and penis dismiss this sexuality as too phallic, as not truly a female sexuality but
rather a copy of male sexuality. We sometimes forget that it was Freud,
over against many of his contemporaries, who recognized the temporal
priority of clitoral orgasms and the difficulty women have in learning to
receive pleasure from vaginal penetration. We need to remember also
that for him vagina (like penis) functions as a metaphor, a metaphor for
a receptive sexuality, indeed, for a receptive, vulnerable, death-accept-

ing way of being in the world. When Freud says that all of us, women and men alike, must learn to overcome our dread of "femininity,"[52] he is in a sense saying, we all need to learn to honor our vaginas! For he regards the move from clitoris to vagina as analogous to the move from narcissism to eros, from the world of fantasy to the social world, from masturbation to intercourse, from death-denial to death-acceptance.

I see us women as lucky in having bodies to help us mark, experience, this distinction—this move to being open to actual others, to love in its deepest sense. I encourage us to amplify our own experience of our vagina, to be open to all it means, not just to its literal physical facticity. I experience my vagina as a passageway to the center of my being, an encouragement to me to be attuned to the inside-ness of things, to mystery. But we must also recognize the ambivalence, the fear as well as longing that this openness to being entered provokes. The vagina is associated with the fact that we are vulnerable in our sexuality, and thus associated with unwelcome penetration, with rape and incest—as fantasies and as painful realities that may effectively separate us from any possibility of enjoying our own sexuality, of feeling that it *is* ours.

The emphasis on the clitoris may mean a valorization of women's *active* desire, a recognition that our sexuality is not simply passive, receptive, responsive. Recognition of our vaginal sexuality may remind us of a complementary truth, the beauty of receptivity and interdependence.

My own solution is to resist the either/or, to affirm instead a pleasurable "both"—or, perhaps even more accurately, an even more pleasurable everywhere! I experience my sexuality as plural, the sites of my pleasure as diffuse. As Irigaray affirms, "A woman's erogenous zones are not the clitoris or the vagina, but the clitoris and the vagina, and the lips and the vulva, and the mouth of the uterus, and the uterus itself, and the breasts."[53] The literalizing restriction of pleasure to particular organs reflects an already-constructed body, a naming whereby particular parts of the body, the "literal" penis or vagina, are imagined as causing pleasure or desire, whereby some organs are deadened to pleasure and others brought to life.[54] Chernin sees "that sad gathering, into a thrust of force, of the body's widespread capacity to delight in its own sensations," as an expression of a kind of tyrannical subduing of the body.[55]

To designate the disruptive, unsettling, Dionysian, nonphallic, intense rapturous pleasure which they exalt as the authentically female expression of sexuality, French feminists have introduced the term *jouissance*. I love the word, partly because of how it sounds, its "juiciness," its evocation of a wet and fluid sexuality, its connotations of a truly playful, joyful sexuality. Like Freud's expansive redefinition of "sexuality" as signifying not just genitality but all our longings for giving and receiving touch and affection, for intimacy, for connection with another, *jouissance* connotes a polymorphous, pleasure-oriented sexuality, a sexuality not defined by erogenous zones, gender differences, reproduction, or orgasmic climaxes. *Jouissance* can be experienced in solitary lovemaking or in lesbian encounters and also in our sexual engagements with men. It frees us from the notion of what *should* happen in any of these engagements, opens us to take delight in what *does* happen. It encourages us to discover our own sexuality, the places on our body we want to have touched, the places on another's we want to touch, the importance we attach to penetration and orgasm and to emotional intimacy with a partner, our feelings about the role that fantasy should play as a prelude, accompaniment, or substitute for physical touch.

Yet I agree with Gallop that somehow, perhaps inevitably, *jouissance* has become a magic talisman, a fetish, for the only authentic sexuality and thus, as she suggests, it has paradoxically been made phallic after all!"[56] How easy it is to put one another down, to judge from a "superior" theoretical position, rather than to listen. And how dreadfully easy to literalize and fetishize any of these understandings of our sexuality. To cling to any one of them as the guarantor of authenticity, rather than to open ourselves to the full metaphorical associations of all and to accept the differences among us. We vary enormously. for instance, in the value we place on orgasms and in whether we have them easily or not. Some of us delight in our capacity for multiple orgasm, in experiencing wave after wave of climactic fulfillment, and valorize this capacity as something that distinguishes us from men. Others of us (or the same ones at different times) see orgasm as almost irrelevant, as associated with a linear goal-oriented male model of sexuality. (Though, let's be honest, there are many men who delight in, even prefer, a more leisurely, gentle, exploratory, dallying sexuality. And let's note also how easy it seems to be in these intramural discussions of female sexuality to label another woman's understanding as too phallic. Maybe we're too ready to see the phallic only in negative terms. I am partnered with a woman who in lovemaking finds it easier to be responsive than initiative taking; unfortunately, the same is true of me. We never long for a penis, but sometimes covet a little more "phallicism"!)

For some of us the real orgasm may not be physical but emotional —the sense of being fully met by another, the sense of being carried out of ourselves at the same time as our partner, the rush of feeling that forces the words I love you past our lips. We experience a loss when the soul connection isn't there. What we value most about sexual ecstasy is the feeling of being in touch with the sacred and transcendent that sometimes accompanies it. The sense of being brought in touch with the core of our own being and of another's. The sense of being most myself because taken away from the separate self defined by will and personal history. The sense of being at one with all that is real and meaningful. The sense of being part of all that is. The "oceanic feeling." The knowledge that the most intense body experience is also the most profound soul experience. Molly Bloom's YES, a yes to this moment and all moments. A yes that continues to reverberate long after the experience that occasioned it is over.

I am fascinated by the language we use in seeking to describe our orgasms to ourselves or to another. So much female erotic writing seems derivative of male erotic writing (like my allusion to James Joyce in the last paragraph) or based on a theory about female eroticism which leads to a reliance on images drawn from nature: waves, tides, meadows, breezes. Sometimes it seems that only a musical score could do justice to the multi-focused experience—the physical sensations, the fullness of emotional feeling, the images that emerge and disappear —and to how our experience varies from one time to another, so that at some times the physical sensations become focal, whereas at others they seem to function primarily as stimulators of a flow of fantasy.

I think we need also to learn to talk to one another honestly about the rhythms and seasons of our desire. I understand so well what Stendhal means when she writes about times of "disillusionment with the body? That too? Desert of sensual pleasure, night of the flesh, its aridity. . . . Meaning dries up, the body withers, scorns touch, grows barren. Someone is in mourning, they say. Perhaps the goddess of grain. Her daughter has been stolen, gone underground."[57] We need to talk about how often we really feel desire. About how open we are to being seduced when we think we don't want to make love. Above all, we need to talk about whether it is all right not to want, about the loss of desire. About whether what we have lost is simply desire for a particular partner or for sex *tout court*. About whether there are changes in the intensity of our desire after menopause. What if cuddling becomes enough—or sharing food, cooking, gardening, hiking, sensual pleasures? So much conspires to make us think we *must* be sexual, but perhaps in this aspect of our life, too, it is appropriate that there be seasons of ebb and seasons of flow.

It is also important for us to talk to one another about our understanding of the relation between female sexuality and reproductive capacity. In my book on menopause I talked about how the Greek traditions about Baubo help us see the continued sexual vitality and juiciness of the postmenopausal crone. When Demeter is grieving the loss of her daughter which she experiences as the loss of her female identity, it is the old peasant woman's lewd dance, culminating in a prideful display of her vulva, which first awakens the goddess to the possibility that there is life after motherhood. In one of his early papers Freud speaks of his hope that someday contraceptives would be developed that might free us to yield fully to desire without the fear of conception. I, coming to maturity in a later time when such contraceptives were available, have certainly rejoiced in the wonderful gift of the freedom to enjoy sex without the fear of untoward consequences.

So, of course, I want to affirm this right to nonreproductive sexual pleasure—yet I would also say that in my own experience subliminal awareness of the link between procreation and sexuality is part of what has given sexual encounters their depth. (I want to be clear here: I believe that a conscious avoiding of conception or a conscious recognition of its impossibility may be a way of honoring, not denying, this link.)

I want also to speak of the sadness that I believe is the usually unspoken accompaniment to deep sexual encounters. The sadness of which Freud so often spoke. The recognition that the transcendence of our separate selfhood we sometimes experience in intercourse is always only a transient moment; but even more deeply the recognition that the bodies through which we experience this ecstasy, this sense of connection, are bodies that will die. A few years ago I spent a night with a man dearly loved for many decades whose body was so injured and weakened we could only with great difficulty enact a simulacrum of our old familiar ways of expressing love. Knowing that it was the last time we would ever do so, we made love in the bittersweet knowledge that someday we would both die but that in the meanwhile we could still touch one another with affection and delight. Less consciously, yet not entirely unconsciously, I believe this awareness underlies all lovemaking.

Birth Giving and Nurturing

I want us also to begin to talk to one another about our wombs, about the pains and joys associated with childbearing and childbirth. In a sense this is an aspect of our embodied experience we have always felt free to talk about. It was never taboo. I remember how at parties during the early years of my marriage the women would often form a group at one end of the room to retell the stories of our deliveries, while the men at the other end talked about football or work. Nonetheless, there are feelings and experiences connected with childbirth we didn't talk about then but need to now.

Precisely because so much conspires to imply that this is the most important aspect of female existence, that the womb in a sense *is* the woman (as the penis is the man), many feminists have strenuously rejected the reduction of women to their reproductive capacity. Indeed, they sometimes even seem to suggest that the only way to be fully woman is to avoid maternity. It is surely true that we are not fully women only if we exercise this capacity. Many of the major Greek goddesses—Persephone, Athene, Artemis, Hestia—were not mothers and yet clearly embodiments of a fully actualized potent mode of female existence.

Yet I sense that all of us are powerfully related to being womb bearers even if we choose not to mother or discover to our sorrow that we cannot. Not just because the culture tells us we should have children but because the not-having is a kind of having, represents a perhaps inescapable relation to the possibility of having. And, I imagine, for all of us, whether we have children or don't, there is always some ambivalence attached to our birth giving capacity: ambivalence about being defined by it, tied down by it, ambivalence about not being able to live it fully or well enough.

Though, as always, each of us can speak only for herself. I have mothered and am grateful that I have. I live with a woman who hoped to have a child and did not. She has accepted that. We have a rich life together. But I suspect she will grieve it always.

I feel (despite all theoretical rejection of the womb/woman equation) that the core of my being is my womb. Where I feel both joy and sorrow most intensely is there, not in heart or belly or head. Merida speaks for me when she writes: "The womb is most maiden in me. Virgin—in herself alone. Integral. Where I am mother is where I am maiden. Not a doubling, not an echoing—but absolute conjunction."[58] What my womb means to me is not only the place within me where I might carry a child but my own withinness. Some who share this feeling speak of their womb as a void waiting to be filled, but my image is more of a plentitude, a fulfilledness. I know that literally as a postmenopausal woman I have a womb not bigger than a walnut, but it still feels as though it is large enough to encompass me, to contain my me-ness. In his essay on the uncanny, on that which is unfamiliar because so overwhelmingly, originally familiar, Freud, too, recognizes the womb as representing for men and women alike the insideness of things, the deep, the unknown, the unconscious, the place of origin and of death.[59]

But what it means will vary. I know the womb can seem a prison for those whose lives are utterly constrained by it, or a place of torture for those who have suffered miscarriages or abortions or hysterectomies.

O Mother, do not again give me a woman's birth
From the beginning there is great suffering for women
O Mother, in the shadow of the twelfth year
My head was found defiled and I was pregnant
The first month is over, Mother
The blood gathers drop by drop
The second month is over, Mother
In the shadow of the third month
My body is as yellow as haldi
And I long for buttermilk
My hands and feet are heavy as earth
I cannot bear the sun
O Mother do not again give me a woman's birth.[60]

To me it is my place, inviolate, but I know that many have had the experience of having even this last resort invaded. By an undesired lover. By a rapist. By an unwanted child. Or by a doctor. How strange, how barbaric in a sense, is the way in which so many female blood mysteries have come to be celebrated in hospitals, with doctors, rather than mothers or sisters or priestesses, in attendance. Because our own longing for success in childbearing has helped lead to the medicalization of conception, gestation, parturition, these most intimate aspects of our lives are today often taken over by physicians, many of whom are men. We chose the change in part—it isn't all something "they" have done to us. We welcomed the anesthesia, the asepsis, the fantasy of a pain-free, risk-free birth process. But as we have realized the full costs of becoming more acted upon than actors, we have begun to try to reclaim birtgiving as a woman's mystery, have turned to midwives, to home births.[61]

My reflections on the role childbearing plays in our lives begin with *conception*. Many associations and images come to mind. The mystery of the hidden, invisible beginning. The conception which is intended and which occurs almost immediately. The conception which is hoped for and after months or years of anticipation finally occurs. The conception which was longed for over many years and finally given up on, but then occurs—almost as a miracle. The conception which was not planned but occurs as a wonderful surprise. The conception which was not planned and is discovered as unmitigated disaster, evoking anger, fear, confusion, despair. The conception which is longed for, hoped toward, worked toward, month after month, but never happens. The conception of a child planned for and welcomed by both parents. The conception of a child where the father seems irrelevant, may not even know of the events, where it is a woman's own blessed secret. The conception of a child forced upon a woman in an act of rape.

I can imagine the very different story that goes with each of these. Some of these stories I have known in my own life, others through the lives of women close to me, others only through fiction or poetry or the daily paper. All seem integral to really understanding what having a womb means. I see each as also opening us to the mysteries of the creative process as it occurs in other domains. How the conception of any decision may take any of these forms, as may the conception of a work of art.

But conception is only the beginning; it is followed by the mystery of *gestation*—the slow growing within our body of another life. This for me was an even greater mystery, the most powerful experience I've known of my body knowing how to perform a miracle about which "I" didn't have a clue —and the experience of coming to feel that the real "I" was precisely the knowing body. The excitement of feeling the changes month by month. The changes in my body's contours and responses. The experience of feeling the new little creature within grow and move and assert its presence. The strange sense of an intimacy of connection to this other who was also still partly myself. The mystery of knowing, more concretely than ever before, that I, too, had begun as a being living within my mother's body.

A friend of mine (who—as part of coming to terms with the fact that this is an experience she will never herself have—has reflected more deeply than any one else I know on what it means to carry a child in one's own body) writes of how pregnancy may trigger this new closeness to one's own mother:

> The woman may experience physical fusion with her infant and metaphorical fusion with her own mother. In pregnancy, she can feel like her mother in this most primal, fundamental and exclusively female way. . . . Pregnancy serves as an effective and natural means to partially satisfy the daughter's desire to return to the primal mother's womb."[62]

But I know it is not always like this. That some pregnancies are physically very uncomfortable. That some are at high risk early on or in the later months. That sometimes the child within feels like an invader. That sometimes it feels as though one's body is betraying one, that more radically than ever before it feels "not-me." And sometimes things go radically wrong—and then there can come a terrible feeling of unworthiness and failure. We're "supposed" to know how to do this and to do it easily and well. This sense of failure may then expand and seem to apply to all of our lives, initiating a crisis of depression and self-denigration and despair. How vulnerable our bodies make us.

I remember still how especially during the first months of my first pregnancy, when I had not yet told anyone that I was expecting, how much I felt, this is *my* mystery—and that of the child within. And yet, of course, it was never only mine. I always knew that eventually others would see and know, whether I said anything or not. But in those first months it was mine to tell, to share. I learned a good deal about myself and about my relationships as I decided whom to tell and when, whom to listen to and whom to disregard among the many ready to tell me how I should be taking care of myself and of my unborn child.

Carrying a child also taught me how strange the whole business of self and other is, how artificial our usual simple divisions. As my child began to grow within my body, I began to see how complex the relation between caring for self and for other is. Sometimes they coincide so closely that we can't really distinguish between them; sometimes they are in painful contradiction, requiring a very delicate act of reconciliation for which neither slogans of maternal selflessness nor of female self-love really help very much.

Conception, gestation, and then: *birth*—the work, the suffering, the risks, the closeness to death, the myths about it that shape how we approach it. For the birth of my child is never the first birth in the world. It always happens in the contexts of the birth stories we've been hearing all our lives, our mother's, our grandmother's, our aunts, our sister's, our best friend's, the peasant woman in the fields, Melanie dying in *Gone With The Wind*, the Lamaze teacher's, the doctor's, the midwife's. And the reality is always different from any of our images. Even when a birth is easy, as mine were, it is nevertheless more frightening, more exhausting, more lonely, more painful than imagined.

And yet I have to say, almost forty years later, that the most sacred moment of my life came when I first held my first child to my breast and felt the mystery of the newness of his being and the mystery of our connection to all the generations that came before and to those that might follow.

My conceptions and pregnancies and births were easy. It was only afterwards that I began to have personal experience of the lesson Carl Kerenyi says we learn from Demeter, "how much of motherhood is loss." (And those later aspects of motherhood I have somewhat arbitrarily chosen to explore in connection with breasts not wombs.) But I know that for many women the primary experience of being a wom(b)an has been loss.

There is infertility. There is miscarriage. There is abortion. There is stillbirth. There is the horror of knowing that one's body may be poisoned (with alcohol, drugs, or AIDS) and may fatally infect our child before it ever emerges from our body. There is giving up a child for adoption. There is having one's womb cut out of one's body.

The *Thesmophoria*, the Demeter ritual which brought Athenian mothers together for a three-day ritual during which they shared with one another the rage and anger provoked by losses such as these, made clear that the losses, too, are part of the sacred events associated with motherhood. The goddess had no power to avert such suffering, but because she had participated in such loss herself, she could help the participants understand how in their shared vulnerability to this suffering woman is bound to woman.

I know something of the pain associated with infertility because I have watched the woman I live with endure that pain. We also have friends who created a ritual to help them move through the process of accepting that they could not conceive so that they might move forward to adopt instead. Watching a film of that ritual has in turn helped other friends suffering the same grief. I have been further helped to understand how powerful a narcissistic wound infertility may inflict by my friend, Jean Thomson. She expresses so clearly how the intense and all-consuming desire for pregnancy is connected to but different from a desire to mother a child, so that adoption is not an answer to *this* longing, though it may answer one's longing to raise a child. There is so much to mourn. The infertile woman loses not just her fantasies of having a child but also her primal identification with her mother and the possibility of her own return to the womb by way of that special bond with her mother. She is *other* than her mother in a primary way, more like a son than a daughter. She may also be cut off from peer women by not participating in the central mystery of their lives. She may lose her sense of having a complete female body, and find herself exposed to the age-old but still continuing debasement of infertile women, viewed as a symbol of death, as a dangerous threat, taboo. Because she loses her access to immortality through participating in the continuity of generations, her infertility may bring her powerfully in touch with her own mortality. She may also discover that after mourning the loss of the possibility of ever bearing a child, it is possible to go on; infertility can teach sublimation, a woman's form of sublimation in which the sublimated libido may be directed into relationship, not necessarily into work, art, achievement. The libido may even be directed toward an adopted child, but to Thomson it is clear that the love directed toward the adopted child represents a *sublimation*, not a direct fulfillment, of the longing to carry a child in one's own body.[63]

Poets (as well as friends) help us enter into such experiences. They help us to live more deeply what we have ourselves experienced but not fully lived and to live imaginatively what we've not literally lived. So, Kathee Miller's poem about miscarriage helps me feel her loss as though it had been written on my own body:

> *death can come pouring down*
> *out of this hole*
> *dead babies can come through*

embryos fetuses tissue blood
thick and scented down into toilets
we hover above
squatted and straining rocking and swaying
between our legs a canyon a flood
emptying out what we were just so full of
but couldn't be seen
no man can feel this miracle this matrix
deep within oneself
holding carrying feeling sensing
seeing with the inner body
what is invisible to the outer eye
and then helpless in agony of loss
one minute full one minute empty
one day life next day death
on and out of this hole
this gateway this matter and space
life giving life destroying,

. . . .

my blood still runs out of me
whose blood is it[64]

Some other cultures provide rituals for helping their members live through the losses mothers and would-be mothers may suffer. I remember visiting the Kwan Yin temple in Yokohama and discovering that most of the young women I saw at the shrine had come to ask the goddess to bless the souls of their unborn children, not only stillborn infants or infants who had died in the first few months of life, but also infants lost to a miscarriage, and, most poignantly to me, infants they had aborted.

Visiting the temple reminded me how difficult it is for many in my culture, who support a woman's right to choose whether to continue a pregnancy or not, to allow room for mourning. In our affirmation of that right, I see us as sometimes tricked into adopting a male model of individual autonomy which isn't always fully compatible with our feelings. And sometimes we act as though we believe that making a rationally defensible choice should protect us from emotional ambivalence. So we may dishonor the loss, the loss of a potential life, the loss of a

part of ourselves, the survivor guilt we may (never mind how irrationally) feel.

We need the poets because we have almost no rituals; we need them
to help us into a grieving which cannot be integrated unless it is first felt,
which cannot be felt unless it is named. I need the poets particularly to
help me into those experiences I have no immediate access to through
my own life story. Yet another poem, this one by Eileen Moeller, makes
me feel that somehow such aborted love must be *the* pain of motherhood:

> *little tadpole*
> *gone back to the ghostworld*
> *I went to the crossroads*
> *could go no further*
> *could go no further*
>
> .   .   .   .
>
> *ten years ago*
> *I bled on a white padded table*
> *and the crone sang her black song*
>
> *and here I am now*
> *still carrying you*
> *question mark curled asleep*
> *in the keening dark of my mouth*
>
> .   .   .   .
>
> *I am still bleeding*[65]

Still another, by Lucille Clifton this time, also moves me deeply:

> *you would have been born into winter*
> *in the year of the disconnected gas*
> *and no car . . .*
>
> .   .   .   .   .   .
>
> *if you were here I could tell you these*
> *and some other things*
>
> *if I am ever less than a mountain*
> *for your definite brothers and sisters*

let the rivers pour over my head
let the sea take me for a spiller
of seas   let black men call me stranger
always   for your never named sake.[66]

Miscarriages, abortions, giving up a child for adoption, still births—and infant death. The death of a young child may perhaps seem even more unfair, more unnatural now than in earlier times because medical technology has made it so much more rare, but always, especially after the first year, it must have been a terrible grief for parents to lose a child. Such a loss seems so radical an overturning of the order of things. I know so many tales of families where the mother never really gets over such a loss, where the child who is dead takes energy from those who live.

I wrote about hysterectomies above while reflecting on the theme of premature menopause, but I would like here, while reflecting on the meanings that having a womb carries for us, to take account of what it may mean to suffer a cervical or uterine cancer. I once thought I might have such a cancer and felt it mysteriously appropriate that I might be carrying death where I have carried life. My friend Merida has had to live as fact what I lived only as possibility. When she first learned of her cancer, she wrote me:

> Have I planted her as I once planted my babies? does she grow from my wishes? my wounds? . . . O gateway to life and death. She opens ferociously, wide and beyond imagining, to life. And now she has opened to this cancer flower. . . . I'm learning that I'm a touchstone for others' terror. Cancer afflicts us all. The fear of contagion. The grief of losses known. I'm charged with the evocative power of this disease. Tomorrow they will take you out. Can you still hear me, sweetie. I croon to you. . . . Tell me all you know, I will remember it always. O, toots, I rub your golden belly lamp, You who have been with me from the beginning. Womb heart of my deepest place. I slip my fingers inside and tickle her. We laugh together. O beauty, oh sweetie, you are more than cells to me. I will have a phantom womb. I will re-member you—as amputees stand on the lost leg.

Later, after her operation, she wrote: "I hold her, hands on my belly, and whisper 'you remember.' "[67]

So much of motherhood is loss. So much of motherhood is hope. As the poet Alta says:

> One hesitates to bring a child into this world without fixing it up a little, paint a special room. stop sexism, learn how to love, vow to do it better than it was done when you were a baby, vow to make, if necessary, new mistakes, vow to be awake for the birth, to believe in joy even in the midst of unbearable pain.[68]

Having wombs reminds us of how much we are part of the ever-ongoing cycle of generations, how much we are used by nature as simply the instrument of her self-continuation. Having wombs reminds us of how much human activity is creative, generative. These other creative activities may in some sense be sublimations of the procreative urge, but such sublimation is required of all of us. Even those of us who have children must at some point stop having them and then learn new ways to channel that energy. Having wombs reminds us of the womb which gave us birth and also, inevitably, of the womb-tomb to which we will return.

I am struck by how in archaic icons of goddesses there is a tendency to emphasize one part of the female body as containing its essence, but (as the illustrations and discussion in Marija Gimbutas's *The Language of the Goddess* make abundantly clear) just which part varies enormously.[69] In some cultures we find enormous emphasis on the pubic triangle, on the goddess's sexuality, in others on her full and prominent buttocks, in still others on her full hips and rounded belly. Sometimes she is clearly pregnant; sometimes she is even represented in the act of giving birth.

At other times it is the goddess's ripe, full breasts that are seen as her most important aspect, or (as in the iconography associated with the Graeco-Roman Isis and the Christian Mary) it is the goddess nursing an infant child that becomes the emblem of female love. I remember vividly the ancient reliefs in the temple at Abydos of Isis holding the adult but child-size Ramesses on her lap; the pharoah, enfolded by the goddess's gorgeous vulture wings, nurses at her breast. And at Hatshepsut's temple near Luxor the female pharoah is shown kneeling under the body of the cow goddess Hathor and suckling at her udder. In Greece we have images of virgin Artemis holding to her breast orphaned fawns and baby wolves. We are told that Hera, the cow-eyed goddess, was tricked into giving suck to the infant Heracles whose birth to a rival she'd done everything in her power to prevent and then delay. Upon discovering the ruse, the goddess angrily pulled the vigorously sucking baby from her breast; the spilled milk, we are told, can still be seen in the heavens as the Milky Way. The Amazons, so the myths about this all-women community relate, cut off one breast so they might be better archers and kept the other so they might nurse their infant daughters.

Much of what we typically associate with motherhood, the years of nurturing care, I see as emerging more naturally out of reflection on our having breasts than wombs. For mothering is more than birth giving. "To give birth is to create a life that cannot be kept safe, whose unfolding cannot be controlled and whose eventual death is certain."[70]

I have come to believe that it may be the birth of a second child that really initiates us into this aspect of motherhood. For as we discover what it is to love two (or more, in my case eventually five) with equal passion and commitment, with the same kind of love, and yet with a welcoming recognition of how different each is in needs and gifts, we truly know how different the love of children is from the love felt for one's one mother, one's one father, or one's one husband.

Our breasts come to carry all the ambivalence we feel toward our culturally assigned role as nurturers—and as sexual objects. I remember how tenderly my friends and I welcomed their first budding appearance—the secret glances, the secret strokes. As though we were somehow giving birth to them. I remember also how reluctant we were to give them public visibility, as though that would be to complete a transition we felt ourselves only beginning to approach. I can also remember a scene that must have taken place about a decade later. Clad only in a bathing suit and proud of my newly almost-flat belly, I was wheeling one of my babies down a seaside boardwalk. Suddenly the baby began to cry and milk started spurting forth out of my nipples in two big arcs right through my bathing suit. I remember how both embarrassed and somehow proud I was. Perhaps my equivalent of a little boy's pride in his arcing pee!

The first meaning breasts have for us is nurturance. We received it (or didn't receive it) from our own mothers, and then if we become mothers ourselves, find ourselves expected to play the role of nurture giver in our turn. Those of us who actually breast-feed our babies (as I did) may receive deep delight from doing so. The closeness of holding the child so recently within our bodies at our breast, feeling the liquid flow from our bodies into theirs, symbolizes that the connection remains. I remember the bliss of feeling the child become satiated, utterly content, and then falling asleep with my nipple still in its mouth—and my own empathic drowsiness. I knew I wasn't supposed to bring my babies into my bed, to let them lie curled against my own recumbent body for those middle-of-the-night feedings, but I couldn't always resist. It was too delicious, too beautiful. I remember, too, the sweetness of their smiles of grateful pleasure when in response to their cries I'd begin to open my blouse, and their eyes so loving fixed on mine as they sucked away.

Even as I write this, more than thirty years since I last nursed a child, I feel the tightening of my nipples, the responding pulse in my vagina. There's a kind of female eroticism around breasts, a from within not a looking-at eroticism, that is as compelling as any I know. A lover sucking at my breasts has great power to arouse me sexually, to fill me with delight in being touched there and with longing to be touched below and entered—but powerful as that lover's touch may be, it does not stir me as deeply as my babies' sucking.

But breast-feeding isn't all bliss. From the beginning it includes an awareness of the tug of the child's otherness and not just of our closeness. It may involve not quite knowing how to do it at first. I remember that when I had my first child, no one I knew had nursed their babies, the doctors discouraged me, the nurses didn't know how to help. I felt very alone and yet I wanted this bond so much. So Peter and I persevered—through cracked and bleeding nipples, engorged breasts, my never being sure I had enough milk. Later, with the others it was easy. They reached for my nipples with a homing instinct as though they knew, yet I understood that it was in part because I now knew.

I loved nursing, yet I also resented it when friends who weren't nursing would explain they couldn't because they weren't as placid as I. (As "cowlike," I think they said, and back then, before I'd come to venerate Hathor, I heard that as an insult.) I could feel my anger rise, as though I was being seen as someone who had no sense of the vitality inherent in more independent, multidimensional ways of being woman. It was painful to discover how vulnerable and resentful I could be at these put-downs by other women. Many men, too, managed to communicate that my nursing was an uncomfortable reminder of our human animality. Another taboo.

So I understand why some women with babies don't breast-feed.

Some feel distaste for the whole idea. Others try but find it's too difficult or truly too painful or that they really don't have enough milk. Getting started can be very trying and can stir up profoundly all our anxieties about being adequate mothers. Or it can stir up the feeling of not wanting to feel ourselves taken over by the mother role, by nurturing, by our breasts. Or perhaps we very much want to nurse our child but have to go to work. In order to be nurturers in the more extensive sense of providers, we have to forego the literal nursing, though we do so with regret. And this difficult choice may come to symbolize our tension around the pulls on us of Demeter and Athene, our conflicted relation to the roles of mother and world maker, how neither role fully satisfies and we don't enact either in a fully satisfactory way.

Or, perhaps most painfully, because we never had a child but longed to, we don't ever get to hold a child to our breasts. And then we may feel they are a wasted, unused part of our body. None of the other ways we find to express our longing to be nurturers may fully satisfy their mute plea to be used. Though, on the other hand, we may also find our work, as teachers or therapists or whatever, satisfies our longing to be nurturers more fully than literal breast-feeding ever could.

Nowadays many women do not nurse and instead rely on bottle feeding, on formulas. Here once again we encounter our ambivalent reliance on medical expertise around what were once recognized as women's mysteries. Wanting to do the best we can for our babies, but not sure we carry the requisite knowledge in our bodies or our heads, we turn for guidance to authorities who are often male. And even if we breast-feed our children, "expert" opinions may inform how we do so. For instance, in my era "demand feeding" was just beginning to be advocated in place of clock-bound scheduling, but it was being imposed in an authoritarian from-outside-a-mother's-bond-with-her-baby way. So we were made to feel guilty if we didn't respond immediately to the new infant's cry. Yet how ridiculous all this became when there was more than one child, and it was obvious that no one person's needs, not the baby's nor the other children's nor one's own, could have any absolute priority, We'd all have to juggle. All have to wait sometimes. All have to be interrupted. And there were no awful consequences.

Eventually there is of course an end to nursing—weaning. And all it brings up, feelings of release but also of regret at the end of a particular bond, a particular kind of closeness, and a particular era in one's life.

Usually weaning stirs up ambivalence, as it may also stir up anxiety about when to wean, a complicating weighing of the interests of one's child, oneself, the rest of the family. I weaned my children early, because I was always ready to have another child soon and after the last was ready to start graduate school (and because it was what women in my world were doing then). Now I see my younger women friends have often not fully weaned their children until they are three or four. Though I know how common this is in most traditional cultures, it is still somewhat strange to me to see these independent, running-off-to-play-with-friends toddlers still returning for a quick gulp at their mother's breasts. And yet I also envy these mothers. And understand their reluctance to let go. I remember nursing my youngest child late at night when everyone else in the family was asleep, and only she and I were awake together, joined in this closest of all bonds. I remember sitting there wondering, night after night, will this be the last time I ever, ever do this? Weaning is difficult, often more difficult I believe for mother than for child—as I've always suspected Persephone's abduction to Hades was more difficult for Demeter than for her daughter. But I know this may be simply the story as I lived it, the perspective of a daughter with a mother more devouring than abandoning, the perspective of a daughter unwilling to be that kind of mother (and yet understanding the pull).

The reference to the myth recalls, of course, that the literal weaning is just that, the literal version of something inherent in motherhood— the coming to terms with loss of which Kerenyi wrote so sensitively. So much of mothering is learning to let go, and yet still care, still be available. How much it involves encouraging an independence that encompasses a recognition of interdependence. (Otto Rank believed teaching that delicate balancing of independence and dependence lies at the very heart of all parenting and mentoring—which was why he thought a therapists's role is really a maternal role.) Many of us may have to recognize that we don't always do this well with our own children. Maybe another later will have to replay the role for them. And perhaps we in turn can do better with the children of others, with our nieces and nephews or with our grandchildren, or our students or patients or readers.

At other times, in other cultures, women who don't nurse their own babies rely on wet nurses. We have all read stories of young children raised by wet nurses who felt them to be their real mothers, stories which often focus on the pain of being torn away from those mothers. But we also know how intensely some adopted children as adults long to reconnect with their birth mothers. Birth giving and nurturing, womb and breast are each an integral but distinct aspect of mothering.

In her book *Maternal Thinking,* Sara Ruddick explores in detail the aspects of mothering distinguishable from birth giving. She does not write about breast-feeding in any literal sense, yet what she has to say about maternal nurturance is much the same as what I feel I learn by reflecting on what it means to me to have a body with breasts. By "maternal thinking," Ruddick says, she means "a kind of lived intelligence," a "hands-on knowing," a thinking that develops from practice, that is developed through the care of children and through taking on the responsibility for their moral and social training. Engagement in this work teaches one to deal respectfully with another human being and to use authority and power benignly. It teaches receptivity to change, awareness of the ebb and flow of feelings, and the capacity to tolerate emotional ambivalence. "Fostering" mothers learn to relish reciprocity, to encounter another as subject and agent, to respond to another's vulnerability. They learn to welcome change and growth, knowing that the point isn't to keep the relationship the same. Much of the work of mothering is simply attentiveness, noting and celebrating and remembering the child's first smile, first step, first word. We learn to allow children their rages, fears, and resentments, and to forgive ourselves for our limitations and failures.[71]

And we do fail. We are too possessive or too self-sacrificing, filled with anxiety or guilt. Sometimes this caring is beyond us; we are tempted to walk away, to throw our children at the wall, to tear off our breasts. Having breasts, being expected to be a nurturer, sometimes seems to ask too much of us.

But breasts signify more than nurturance; they are also sexual symbols. Perhaps they evoke sexual desire *because* they once provided the sustenance on which our life depended. Freud suggests that *all* sexual pleasure may be "anaclitic," derivative of our first experiences of sensual pleasure, nursing at our mother's breast. I have written already of how the experience of having a child suck at our breasts may reconnect us to that primal experience, may recall our ecstatic fusion with her. And nursing itself is also profoundly sexual, as I also said above. As is having our breasts stroked and kissed and sucked upon by a lover. As is caressing and sucking the breasts of a woman lover and feeling that eerie sense of our each being both nurser and nursling. We can easily understand why men are so pulled to our breasts, how to suck on them may in fact be more profoundly evocative of incest longing than intercourse itself.

Yet just because of that, because of how breasts suggest fusion longing, the pull to the breast may be felt as dangerous, as threatening the loss of the subject position, the loss of autonomy and agency. And so the pull is transposed into a different key, is converted into a more objectifying appreciation. Breasts become something to look at. And our breasts become something seen. Seen by men, by other women, by ourselves. So that we, too, are encouraged to look at our breasts as though from outside. As fetish not function. And a whole new set of anxieties are introduced. Are they too big or too small? Too round or too droopy? We dress to emphasize them, to make them fit the cultural norm. Some of us may even resort to augmentation or reduction. We may decide not to nurse because preserving their maidenlike firmness, the pinkness of their nipples, seems more important. We want them to be *our* breasts (or our lover's) rather than our child's. Breasts are the visible sign of our femininity, unlike wombs whose presence is hidden. In a sense they rather than the clitoris are the female equivalent of the penis (as Freud saw in his essay on Leonardo)—they even get erections!

Thus the loss of a breast has all the force of a castration wound. To lose one breast or both brings up the many associations we have with what it means to have breasts. A mastectomy is not just the loss of a body part but the loss of these functions, these capacities, these pleasures, these beauties—and it is painfully difficult to let go of the identification of these meanings with the body part that symbolizes them. To believe that I am still fully female, still capable of nurturance, still beautiful, still sexual, without my breast. And it is painful, too, not to have the full range of meanings recognized. To have the assumption be that it is primarily the breast-as-seen (which can at least in part be replaced by surgery or a prosthesis) whose loss we grieve— when what we really mourn is so much more, the breast-from-within.

Aging and Dying

The loss probably means differently, and I would guess more, to women who suffer it before menopause than after. But then everything looks different later, when what attending to the body means is attending to its aging. I have written about the early stages of that process in my book on menopause and return to the theme in the next chapter. As I write there, aging may not make us wise or brave or powerful— but it makes us ourselves. As May Sarton writes:

> *Now I become myself. It's taken*
> *Time, many years and places;*
> *I have been dissolved and shaken,*
> *Worn other people's faces. . . .*
> *All fuses now, falls into place*
> *From wish to action, word to silence.*
> *My work, my love, my time, my face*
> *Gathered into one intense*
> *Gesture of growing like a plant.* [72]

The last of these female blood mysteries is, of course, the mystery of death. The acknowledgment that we are embodied souls, en-souled bodies, helps prepare us for the inevitability of our death. All the particular aspects of our female embodiment, having periods and having them cease, giving birth to children at risk of death, nurturing children who will grow up to leave us, bring us in touch with change and loss, with finitude and death. The soul experiences our bodies expose us to connect us to the tragedy of life—remind us that there is no real overriding of that tragedy through reason or spirit, only a way *into* it, a descent. Attending to the meanings implicit in our embodiment as we have sought to do in this chapter issues in an affirmation of life as lived on earth and of our interdependence with all other life. It may teach us what Carol Christ sees as the most important lesson of all: "To learn to love this life that ends in death."[73]

The arrows of Artemis, the same goddess who presides over all the other female body mysteries, bring death to women. The Eleusinian mysteries celebrated in honor of Persephone, goddess of the underworld, release us from fear of death, not from death. That it is a goddess who presides over the realm of the dead means that the Greeks (like many others) saw death as a female mystery—but Persephone welcomes the souls of all who have died to her realm, men and women alike. Attunement to death as a part of life is available to men as well as to women, as are all these insights about human life and our relation to the natural world garnered through reflection on particular aspects of the female body. Having direct access to that body may make women more open to these insights, though I don't think that matters much. What does matter is that all of us begin to take seriously modes of consciousness which accept change, interdependence, and death.

·5·

RITES OF ANCIENT RIPENING

W hat does matter is that all of us begin to take seriously modes of consciousness which accept change, interdependence, and death. I keep returning to this theme. I keep approaching it from new directions. This book begins with an evocation of what I learned from someone whom I encountered in my youth as the epitome of the wise old woman, Esther Harding. In the interval I have had many other teachers, Freud and Jung, Artemis and Aphrodite, the matristic past and contemporary women friends like Carol Christ and Karen Brown, my dreams and my female body. Now I am nearly as old as Harding was when I met her and understand from within that wisdom and age are more paradoxically related than I realized when I was young. I do know though that I am fast moving into the phase of a woman's life traditionally associated with the figure of the Crone and that whatever wisdom I may have to share comes from my ever deepening conviction that these are my themes: change, interdependence, and death.

For the last decade I have been a postmenopausal woman. My passage through menopause was presided over by a wise old woman who seemed to have leapt straight from the pages of the Grimms' *Household Tales* into one of my own dreams. Bent and wizened and utterly confident, she led me through a moonlit ritual whose very existence had been unknown to me.[1] Now almost ten years later, in my inner life *She* is still the Crone, not I.

The Figure of the Crone

Crone—the very word stirs up profound ambivalence in me. On the one hand I feel myself unworthy of this designation—not wise enough, not completed enough, not old enough, not transcendent enough. On the other I feel myself still too powerful, too active, too happy and healthy to be her. Not yet, not yet.

Maiden, Mother, Crone—the more I reflect on this trinity the more elusive it becomes. At first it seems to refer to three stages of female life, which in less mythological language we might call adolescence (the prepubertal years somehow become erased, as though in childhood we are not really *female* yet), maturity (the years when a woman's existence is stereotypically ordered toward sexuality and motherhood), and old age (or the postmenopausal years). But this doesn't quite fit after all. Maiden evokes some aspects of female experience that are not fully experienced in adolescence and that are actually part of our lifelong sense of ourselves, and the same is true of Mother and Crone.

I have remembered all these years how, during my thirties, a man, who had initially been drawn to me by the sophistication and sexual allure I seemed to embody, later told me that what he had really come to delight in most was the playful little girl he had discovered me still to be, what he had come to value most was the wise old woman who appeared from time to time. All three in some sense coexist within us all along, and perhaps we feel fully known only by those who are able to discern their copresence. I have been struck by how my parents in their eighties feel closer to the friends of their youth (with whom they had almost no contact after we left Germany in 1935 until a decade or so ago) than to the American friends among whom they have lived for over fifty years; they seem to feel that only those who knew them when they were becoming who they are can understand who they are now.

In a sense the Maiden represents an irrecoverable (because never literally possible) innocence, inviolability, self-sufficiency; the Crone a longed-for but to some degree unrealizable attainment of a fulfilled wisdom and power. But I'm not happy with a view that focuses only on the positive side of the archetype and ignores the confusion, loneliness, vulnerability, and emptiness of the Maiden, and the incompletion, impotence, vulnerability of the Crone. Such avoidance of the darker side seems to occur when we allow archetypes to exist independently of actual lives—or of actual myths. Somehow we need to explore how the fantasies we have about the Crone, the myths handed down about crones, and the actual experience of old age by contemporary women interrelate.

I am going to use Crone as meaning Old Woman—old woman as represented in our fantasies (both hopeful and fearful), old woman as represented in mythology (particularly the Greek mythology I know best) and old woman as contemporary old women describe their own experience. I will be attending particularly to the latter and less to mythological testimony. As I indicated in my book on menopause there are actually very few Greek myths about old women. There are groups of ancient female figures (the Moirae, the Erinyes, the Keres, the Harpies) and a few individual females who are little more than abstract personifications (Nyx, Ananke, Nemesis), but the traditions about these old women of myth tell us little beyond the fact that the Crone was associated by the Greeks with the implacable forces of destiny, the inescapability of a transhuman earth-based justice, and the inevitable coming of death. Though all were viewed as fearful and often represented as frightful in appearance, they were not regarded as unjust or malign. The Crone simply represents the passage from life to death. For a more articulated understanding of how the Crone enters into our inner lives I have found myself in tutelage to my mother and to the written accounts of other older women. I have come to believe that the She from whom I learn what I most need to know is likely to be not a goddess or my inner Self but other living women.[2]

I will be trying to discover more clearly my own relation to being and becoming an old woman, to look at the sense in which I have been one (known one to live within me) for decades, the sense in which since I went through menopause I am one now, the sense in which my mother is one and I am not yet, the sense in which one never fully becomes *Her*.

When I was Maiden, I hardly knew it. My recognition of the ways in which my personal struggles echoed age-old archetypal patterns came mostly retrospectively, as I sought to honor the continued presence in me of the maiden or (perhaps better) *virgin* (in Esther Harding's sense of in-one-selfness) at a time when outwardly I seemed to be identified with the Mother. From the perspective of the Mother, the Maiden is seen as all prospect: she is full of anticipation, of looking forward; she represents female existence *before* it is in touch with dimensions of experience central to the Mother phase: *before* sexuality, *before* birth giving, *before* engagement with the underworld. Though actually when one *is* Maiden, it is never so innocent a state of being. One may already be all too familiar with underworld reality, one may find oneself just as defined by relationships (or by the pain of their inadequacy or absence) as later on. The idealization of the Maiden is the Mother's—who, looking back, in a sense creates the Maiden as emblem of an aspect of her own self whose loss she mourns or whose fragile persistence she fiercely defends. Persephone's innocence is Demeter's fantasy.

When I was outwardly, chronologically Mother, I both affirmed and fought against that designation, celebrated the fulfillments that came with birthing and helping to raise my five children and yet experiencing "Mother" as both too grandly archetypal and too personally constraining.

But my disavowal of the Crone feels different—as though the disavowal were itself integral to what this archetype implies, requires, gives and withholds. Perhaps to fully acknowledge one's identity with Her would be to die? I believe that my disavowal is not mine alone. I see my mother, almost ninety, still warding Her off. As I read the accounts of women much older than I, attempting to articulate their experience of being seventy, eighty, ninety, I discover how for them, too, there is acknowledgment of the Crone, and denial. Perhaps this is because the Crone is inherently a transcendent figure. (The Greeks, I recall, recognized old age as specifically *liminal*, as embodying the threshold between life and death, not so much as a final stage of life as the passage away from life.)[3]

She stirs ambivalence in us. Women of my age inevitably remember the negative connotations "crone" and its analogues—"hag" and "witch," "harpy," "shrew," "virago"—used to evoke. These words referred to ugly old women, to repulsive and terrifying women who were in compact with evil spirits., to the primordially "other." We have celebrated the reclaiming of the language, of these words, by such feminists as Mary Daly and Barbara Walker. We have learned to apply these terms proudly to ourselves, as African-Americans have learned proudly to proclaim themselves as blacks and some of my gay friends choose to call themselves faggots. We enjoy Walker's deriving "hag" from *hagia*, the Greek word for the holy rather than from an Old English word for "hedge"; we are ready to second Daly's interpreting "crone" by way of the Greek *khronios*, "long lasting." These playful etymologies are illuminating; the ones given in our usual dictionaries may indeed betray some bias. How can one know so surely that "crone" comes from an Old Dutch word for "old ewe," "dead body," and ultimately from *carn*, "flesh," but that "crony" (an "intimate companion," presumably male) derives from *khronios*. (Whereas "crone" is officially denied any connection to *khronios*, much is often made of the playful etymology which associates *khronios* with Kronos, the Greek Titan, who is viewed as epitomizing the Senex, the male equivalent of the Crone.)[4] It is interesting that Crone *seems* to have an entirely distinct etymology.

The revisionings have encouraged us to think of crones as long-lasting survivors, as wise and powerful, self-affirming women, as wanton, willful, intractable women, as women who refuse to yield to patri-archal power and thus represent all that men find terrifying in indepen-dent women.⁵

Yet there is something too simple in this positive feminist view of the Crone. It equates the Crone with the rejected feminine, with the power of women-identified women which men find frightening and ugly and consequently calumniate and vilify, but it doesn't seem really fully to recognize the Crone as the *old* woman. Walker makes clear that by "crone" she means socially active "elder women," women beyond "their young-mother" years, women of "middle age and beyond"; Daly that she means to emphasize "the intractable spirit" not the age of crones and hags.⁶ The sense we get is that the Crone is woman as resolutely *not*-mother, perhaps *never*-mother, at the least *after*-mother. These women, more or less my contemporaries, are proud to call themselves crones, but in a way that seems to ignore the realities of true old age—and the dark side of the Crone archetype. I find myself suspicious of these midlife Crones. I'm less sure than they that only men are frightened of the Crone, for I believe She may represent something in ourselves that frightens us—and that we avoid by claiming that we are already crones.

I find myself nodding in agreement when Laurel Rust writes, "I feel that in feminist circles, when the subject of women and aging comes up, [actual older] women, especially those who cannot or do not communi-cate or relate to 'reality' as we do, are very often forgotten despite all the adulation of hags and crones."⁷ I value Sandra Scofield warning of the dangers inherent in the "urgent desire to find old age a happy part of life's cycle" and thus to ignore the faults, the bitterness, the regrets of old women.

The result is sentimental, cloying, and, I suspect, false. I want to know how the old absorb their losses, how they look back on lost opportu-nity and bear disappointments in their family and friends. I want to know how they live with their dark sides.⁸

Writing this book serves as an occasion for looking back over the last decade and reviewing what I had earlier anticipated might lie ahead. As I first entered this final third of a woman's life, the years after meno-pause, I imagined that more of my energies would henceforward be devoted to my relationships with women, and particularly the woman with whom I had just begun to live (and still—joyfully and effortlessly —live). I had expected that I would be pulled more to reflection and introversion than to further outward achievement. I had foreseen that preparation for death would become a more conscious task than in earlier years.

The actuality has been different. Perhaps it always is. May Sarton writes of how different being seventy is from how she had imagined it when sixty:

> These previews of old age were not entirely accurate, I am discovering. And that, as far as I can see, is because I live more completely in the moment these days, am not as anxious about the future, and am far more detached from the areas of pain, the loss of love, the struggle to get work completed, the fear of death. I have less guilt because there is less anger.[9]

I had a similar experience when I realized how different my actual journey through menopause was from my expectations:

> My preparations seemed in large measure irrelevant, except that they had opened me to live the menopausal transition consciously and symbolically. Where I had hoped to have communion, I found myself undertaking a radically solitary journey; where I had expected to be immersed in feminine reality, I found myself engaged in a struggle with the masculine; where I had anticipated being taught by dream and myth, I found myself learning from strangers, events and landscapes met in an outer though utterly unfamiliar world.[10]

And now again I recognize how different these most recent years have been from what I had thought likely. I *have* been deeply involved with women and with a particular woman; indeed, this relationship, especially during its first years, has been more demanding and more difficult than I ever anticipated. I *have* been more deeply engaged with death than at any earlier period, but *not* so much with my own as with the threatened death of the HIV-positive gay men I love. But this has *not* been a period of reflection rather than achievement; instead, it has been a time of an unprecedented rush of creative, productive energy. I am surprised by that, grateful for it, and a little embarrassed, too—as though I *should* be done with that by now. Again Sarton consoles, as she admits how much difficulty she still has in balancing the inner and outer: "If I had imagined this year as one with time for reflection, it is always a mistake to try to order one's life in such an arbitrary way. Time for reflection will come when time is ripe."[11]

Thus it seems important to be honest about where I am now: sixty, not seventy as Sarton was when she wrote this, not over eighty as Florida Maxwell-Scott was when she wrote *The Measure of My Days*, not almost ninety like my mother. There are valid reasons for my resisting the relevance of the Crone archetype to *me*. Indeed, I am struck by the resentment some "real" crones feel at the readiness of midlife women to speak authoritatively about old women. Baba Copper, for example, says of the midlife woman "rushing forward to define the problem:" "In asserting her power over the insights of the old woman . . . she unconsciously silences the inherent radicalism of the only one who can tell her how it really is."[12] Shevy Healey agrees, "When discussion of aging begins and remains primarily about women in their 40s and 50s, it reinforces the invisibility of the old woman, and diminishes the importance of the last 25 years of life."[13] Sarton, implying that "real" old age is something she has yet to experience, says she believes that "real old age begins when one looks backward rather than forward," and that at seventy she is still looking "forward with joy to the years ahead,"[14] But I suspect that is too simple; that all the way through we look in both directions.

I am fully aware of the differences between myself and women decades older than I. Not yet retired, I am still inwardly deeply involved with my work as a teacher and still outwardly defined by the social status it confers. Although I have deep facial wrinkles, a flaccid belly, a few grey hairs, I have little experience yet of physical diminishment or chronic pain. I know this is a boon not to be counted on by one of my age. Adrienne Rich, only a few years older than I, knows well what it is to be "signified by pain":

> *The problem, unstated till now, is how*
> *to live in a damaged body*
> *in a world where pain is meant to be gagged*
> *uncured un-grieved over*[15]

And Audre Lorde, only a few years younger than I has lived through two bouts of life-threatening cancer and learned from them that "as a living creature" she is "part of two kinds of forces—growth and decay, sprouting and withering, living and dying," intent on "trying to find what my body wants to do."[16]

I certainly have little experience yet of the most important losses that older women emphasize: the loss of a familiar body, the loss of friends, losses which in sum comprise the loss of one's world. Rich writes powerfully of what it is like to engage in such "acts of loss":

> It's true, these last few years I've lived
> watching myself in the act of loss—the art of losing,
> Elizabeth Bishop called it, but for me no art
> only badly-done exercises
> acts of the heart forced to question
> its presumptions in this world its mere excitements
> acts of the body forced to measure
> all instincts against pain
> acts of parting trying to let go
> without giving up[17]

Thus I see clearly the inappropriateness of a premature identification with the Crone. Yet I also see the dangers in denying that identification. It feels important to look honestly at what is being avoided in such denial. The same women who write so passionately against younger women's usurping their right to define old age protest vigorously against the self-deceptions involved in "passing" for younger than one is. As Copper puts it:

> Age passing—passing for young enough—is part of all female experience. The foundation of lies built into passing and the fear and loathing of female aging are what keeps the generations of women—decade by decade—divided from each other.
>
> I believe that age passing is one of the primary learning arenas of female competition, as well as an apprenticeship to hatred of old women. When women pass easily, we gain comfort knowing that we do not have to identify with the woman who, in our view, is not passing. "I am not like her" translates easily into "I am better than her." . . . Somewhere in our fifties. the mass of anxieties about age, and the increase of rejection and invisibility we are experiencing, becomes critical. This is often a time when our trained inability to identify with women older than our-

selves reaches its climax. . . . The midlife woman, in her rage and fear, may unconsciously discharge all kinds of covert aggression against the old woman as the personification of what is threatening her.[18]

Again Healy echoes her:

In my late fifties, and then my sixties, I heard, "I can't believe you're that old. You don't look that old."At first that felt like a compliment. Then I became a bit uneasy. It reminded me of early pre-feminist days when I was complimented by some men for being "smarter," "more independent" than those "other" women."[19]

So I realize I need to ask what fear, what rage, what misogyny am I hiding from in regarding the Crone as other?

I imagine it is hard for any woman with a still living mother to take quite seriously her own identification as a Crone. I was struck last summer when I went to a gathering of "crones" to find that almost all were about my age—but that what most of us wanted to talk about was our mothers! I have found this true of so many of the deep conversations I have had with my contemporaries—we are engaged with our relation to our mothers as we have not been since we became mothers ourselves. And what so many of us voice is: first, concern with the unhappiness, the rage, the helplessness, and the resented dependence on us evidenced by so many of our mothers; second, but somehow even more forcibly, our fear of becoming them. Where once we may have said, "I don't want to grow up to be like her," now we find ourselves saying, "I don't want to grow old like her."

We know that is not rational; *I* know it's not rational. I have made very different decisions in my life from those my mother made in hers. There is little likelihood that I would feel the same anger at gifts not actualized, at recognition not received, at status not acquired, at a life partner for whom I'd "sacrificed" my life, that fuels my mother's obsessive litany. I feel deep empathy for her; I understand that her rage is one that feminist analysis justifies—yet it terrifies me. Partly because I can do nothing to assuage it. To confirm her view of the real tragedy in her life seems only to keep her more mired in her sorrow and anger. To remind her of how creative her life *has* been—to name not only how much it has been her generosity, her imaginative gaiety, her hope-giving confidence that has so positively shaped the lives of her children and grandchildren and great-grandchildren, but also to recall the more than three thousand poems she has published, the AAUW fellowship named in her honor for the work she did to encourage the creative and scholarly activity of younger women—is not to honor the not-enough-ness of how this feels to her now. To suggest that the regretted shape of her life is in part the consequence of choices *she* made, not entirely due to what Hitler or her husband or her mother-in-law imposed on her, makes no sense to her and is not something she is willing to explore. She is losing her vision and rightfully rages at the dependence that causes. She cannot read her own mail, cannot write her own checks, does not recognize faces when she is greeted on the street. She can hardly read her own typing and so feels robbed of what has been her primary expressive and creative outlet all her life, writing letters and poems. She is stubborn; she wants it to be, herself to be, as she *was*.

I feel for and with her, and I am angry at her—for being unhappy, but really because I am afraid I will become her. I am so aware of how even now she is *in* me—in my body, in my gait, my smile, my frown, my gestures, not so much in facial resemblance as in the *expressions* that somehow feel even more personal than the shape of my nose or the color of my eyes. She is already in me—perhaps someday she will take me over.

I know many other old women, some of whom seem much happier than my mother. I am moved and impressed by the creativity into advanced old age of women like Meridel LeSueur, Georgia O'Keeffe, Louise Nevelson, Martha Graham; although I am also aware of not knowing as much as I would want to of their *inner* experience of being old, of their more difficult moments with it (though I am sure there have been such moments).

Nevertheless, *the* exemplar of the Crone for me remains my mother. I am struck by the truth of James Hillman's observations:

> The mother-complex is basic to our most permanent and intrac-table feelings. In this sense the mother is, as Jung said, fate. This complex is the permanent trap of one's reactions and values from earliest infancy, the box and walls in every situation which-ever way one turns. One faces the mother as fate, ever again and anew. . . . The way we feel about our bodily life, our physical

self-regard and confidence, the subjective tone with which we take in or go out into the world, the basic fears and guilt, how we enter into love and behave in closeness and nearness, our psychological temperature of coldness and warmth, how we feel when we are ill, our manners, taste, and style of eating and living, habitual structures of relating, patterns of gesture and tone of voice, all bear the marks of the mother. . . . The mother-complex is not my mother, it is my complex. It is the way in which my psyche has taken up my mother. Behind is the *Magna Mater.*[20]

But somehow as one approaches old age disentangling the personal mother from the archetype, from the Crone, becomes difficult again. I thought I had done *that* long ago. But it is still there to be done again.

Not only so that I can establish my own relation to the Crone, but that I can stop projecting onto my mother and onto other older women what really belongs to the Crone. Barbara Macdonald has written passionately of her resentment at how younger (including midlife) women tend to look to old women as mothers or grandmothers. She believes that by assuming the daughter role in relation to women older than ourselves, we participate in an ageism that has its roots in the patriarchal family. We are pulled into a male definition of the mother as there to serve us, as though serving us were her purpose in life. "This infantilizes you and it erases me":

> The old woman is at the other end of that motherhood myth. She has no personhood, no desires or values of her own. She must not fight for her own issues—if she fights at all, it must be for "future" generations. . . . You who are younger see us as either submissive and childlike, or as possessing some unidenti-fied vague wisdom. As having more "soul" than you or as being over-emotional and slightly crazy. As weak and helpless or as a pillar of strength. . . . You pity us, or ignore us—until you are made aware of your ageism, and then you want to honor us. I don't know which is worse. None of these images has anything to do with who we are—they are the projections of the oppres-sor. . . .
>
> You come to old women who have been serving young women for a lifetime and ask to be served one more time. . . . But let me say it to you clearly: We are not your mothers, your grandmothers, or your aunts.[21]

Macdonald suggests that "Grandmother" becomes the "safest identity" for an old woman—because it forestalls her being identified as the "Evil Old Woman," as "the loathsome witch who cares only for herself and poisons and devours the young," who represents "the fear of woman as existing not only to create and nurture others but to create and nurture her Self."[22]

In a similar vein Healey writes of the oppression of old women inherent in the expectation that they be content:

> The oppressed old woman is required to be cheerful. but if you're smiling all the time, you acquiesce in being invisible and docile, participating in your own "erasure." If you're not cheerful, then you are accused of being bitter, mean, crabby, complaining. A real Catch-22![23]

These women warn us against projecting wisdom or beneficent power on them, just as ardently as they admonish us not to identify them with weakness or ugly, destructive power. They suggest that perhaps these apparent opposites are in reality but two sides of the same evasion of the actualities of old women's self-understanding. Yet perhaps at the archetypal level, it is not so much that *neither* is true but that both are, that what we need to do is to look at the wisdom and ignorance, the power and vulnerability, the peace and rage, the generosity and selfishness, of the Crone—and at Her distance from and closeness to us.

The Ambivalent Gifts of Aging

In her simple and wise book, *Old Age,* Helen Luke writes of the three gifts reserved for the old: the bodily changes, helpless rage, and memory. She acknowledges that it may sometimes be difficult to remember that these things are "gifts."[24] Perhaps it is precisely the way in which each is blessing *and* curse that makes them so profoundly relevant to our understanding of what constitutes the full meaning of the Crone archetype. The Crone's body, Her relation to death, Her power, Her rage, Her wisdom, and Her memories—these are the themes which engagement with Her bring to the fore.

I find myself going back to the etymology, to the "official" one which links "crone" to an Old Dutch word for "old ewe" or "dead body"; then tracing it back to the Latin *carn*, "flesh," sees it as cognate with "carnal," "carnival," and "incarnate." I like this recognition that crones are *embodied*, this suggestion that we cannot do justice to who the Crone is unless we associate Her with Her aging body, and expect that Her soul-state will be related to Her body-state.

This, like so much else, is two-edged. We women have been socialized to attach much significance to our body's appearance, and thus may find accepting our body's aging difficult; we may invest much energy in trying to inhibit the appearance of wrinkles or disguise the appearance of grey hair. No matter how feminist we are, most of us have introjected some of these messages about our bodies. And yet if we seek to modify our bodies to meet our own standards, we may "achieve instead an awful estrangement from our own bodies."[25] Obviously I am better off in those moments when I can become genuinely interested in the physical changes occurring in my body: the brown spots that cover my arms and chest, the prominent veins on my hands, the facial lines that record my anxieties and my delights, the skin hanging loose on my upper arm, the flat and flaccid buttocks, the thinning pubic hair. Barbara Macdonald moves me deeply with how naturally she seems able to do this:

> "I like growing old," I say to myself with surprise. I had not thought that it could be like this. There are days of excitement when I feel almost a kind of high with the changes taking place in my body, even though I know the inevitable course my body is taking will lead to debilitation and death. I say to myself frequently in wonder, "This is my body doing this thing." I cannot stop it, I don't even know what it is doing. I wouldn't know how to direct it. My own body is going through a process that only my body knows about. I never grew old before, never died. I don't really know how it's done.[26]

This reminds me of how I felt when I was pregnant: an awe at my body's knowledge of how to do this, an awe I have also felt about menstruating, orgasm, nursing, but had not thought to feel about aging until I read these words! My body knows how to do this: it will teach me.

But such acceptance, as Helen Luke sees clearly, is not easily won:

Sight may grow dim, or hearing less acute; taste, smell and touch may lose their power to delight us. Many activities on which we have depended become impossible. Such losses may deprive us of much of the "enchantment" which we have taken for granted as a channel of meaning. . . . For the creative person this loss of perception through the senses may be an even greater threat, a separation between body and soul that strips meaning from both.[27]

A friend of mine, a woman of my own age, had a dream which communicates this very powerfully:

Six of us, all middleaged women were to be tortured on a medieval torture rack. But somehow five of us managed to free ourselves, only the sixth one agreed to the rack. I was pleased with myself that I would not have to face the pain.

She continued the dream in active imagination:

I sought out the torturer to find out why we were to be tortured. Somehow I thought the torturer would be a man but to my surprise an old woman appeared. Her face was partially veiled by a black robe which could have been a nun's habit or a witch's cloak. . . . I asked, "Who are you?" and she replied, "I am what I am. I am neither good nor evil. I serve both life and death. I am at home in the darkness."

"But why do I have to be tortured?" I asked. And she answered, "To know me, you must be willing to endure pain and through death gain new life. You want to be free, but are you truly free when you have fear? Who is more in bondage, the woman who willingly submits to change or the one who runs away?"

Her words shook me to the core. The demon-witch tells me in order to gain new life, I must be willing to submit to the stretching and shrinking of the personality, to face my own extinction. I must be willing to face the fears of growing old with all its limitations, the gradual giving up of youthful looks, ambitions, dreams of power, visions of riches, and eventually life as lived before, and to be receptive only to what is.[28]

My friend's experience is echoed in Luke's recognition of how close body and soul are, how the loss of physical energy entails "the seeming loss of what has seemed most valuable to our souls, when all emotional experience of the numinous has faded."[29] Somehow the acceptance we may indeed achieve may cohabit with regret, regret based on something much deeper than just identification with youthful attractiveness and sexual allure— the regret at being mortal. The body that knows how to age is a body preparing to die. In the last pages of her book Macdonald writes of her initially enraged response to a worrisome cataract:

> I felt betrayed by my own body that had always protected me. . . . My body was not only not taking care of me; it no longer knew how to operate the whole internal, unseen, magical show any more. For the first time in my life, I was afraid of it.

Soon she begins again to feel that she and her body belong together, that it is all she has, and that together they would have to see it through:

> I begin to understand that my body is still in charge of my life process and has always been. It is still taking good care of me, but it has always had two jobs: to make sure that I live and to make sure that I die. . . .
> With the deep knowledge with which it has always protected me—now even against my will, it turns my sights toward an inner world.[30]

The old woman not only has to come to her own terms with her own oncoming death—but also with the way she is viewed as a representative of death, as death bringer. There is something both right and wrong about this. As Healey describes, old women become a carrier of our culture's death taboo:

> The assumption that death is a preoccupation, or subject of expertise, of midlife or old women is ageist. . . . The old should not be seen as standing with death at their elbow. Nor should they be expected to help others on the subject or allow the subject to be age segregated. . . . Death is a forbidden subject with all but the old, who are expected to carry the burden of this social oppression."[31]

As if only old people die—which as I watch my gay friends struggle with AIDS, I certainly know is not true. Yet old woman after old woman testifies to the discovery that the appropriate task of old age is "to learn to live with loss and death, to prepare for my own death. . . . To face the challenge of dying with grace—that is power."[32]

Walker sees the projection of death fear as true of *men's* imaginings of the old woman; she sees it as representing the "symbolic feminization of man's ultimate fear: the fear of his final non-existence"; the fear of the "common garden-variety of death"—not the hero's sudden, violent, "glorious" death, but "death from wasting disease, death after slow degeneration of body and mind." The death-bringing Crone becomes in the male imagination a castrator, most vividly imagined as a "collector of severed penises."[33]

But I believe the Crone plays this role in *women's* imaginings as well —and furthermore that we *need* images of death, images which honor our fear of death as well as our acceptance. Walker recognizes that for women the Crone may be associated with ancient images of benevolent goddesses who welcome and protect women in the land of the dead. She reminds us of how in traditional cultures elderly priestesses in the service of the destroyer aspect of the goddess prepare the ill for death, preside over the rites of mourning, and guide the spirits of the dead to the afterworld.[34] I find this image of women as unambiguously reconciled with death as too simple. It may be true that we women have an *easier* time accepting our human participation in the natural cycles of life, death, and renewal than do men, but I'm not persuaded it is *easy* even for us. Macdonald claims that in Sarton's *As We Are Now* the source of the old woman's power is that she is not afraid to die—but to my mind the novel shows how hard won that fearlessness is.[35] Much of the power of Audre Lorde's account of her wrestling with liver cancer comes from her acknowledgment of the months of denial, the moments of rage and despair, as well as from the account of eventually coming to a "wish to live whatever life I have as fully and sweetly as possible."[36]

I am interested in the very many different ways women die, in those who go gentle into the dark night and those who refuse to. Lorde writes of preparing to write her own "Book of the Dead":

> I keep observing how other people die, comparing, learning, critiquing the process inside of me, matching it up to how I would like to do it. And I think about this scrutiny of myself in the context of its usefulness to other[s]. . . . I think of how important it is for us to share with each other the powers buried within the breaking of silence about our bodies and our health,

even though we have been schooled to be secret and stoical about pain and disease.[37]

I suspect that the longing for the Crone to mean a fully worked-through acceptance of death is connected to the persistent fantasy of the possibility of a truly *completed* life. I have watched the power of this fantasy over my parents, as they communicate how painful for them it is when one or another of their children or their nine grandchildren are going through a time of confusion. They want so much to have everything be in place before they die. Carolyn Heilbrun believes this fantasy has particular power over women:

> We Women have lived too much with closure. . . . There always seems to loom the possibility of something being over, settled, sweeping clear the way for contentment. This is the delusion of the passive life.[38]

I, too, have begun to realize how important it is to get past the sense of life as closure, of death as closure on something rounded off.

Embracing the Crone, making Her our ally—seems in so many ways to be more difficult than we might wish. We want so much affirmation from Her that in the end it will be easy. We want Her to stand before us not only as a woman fearless before death but as a woman powerful in life. Yet as I have already suggested, I have deep reservations about an emphasis on the Crone's *power,* especially when we forget how much of the Crone's peculiar power lies in Her acknowledgment of weakness and of need for others, and of Her *hatred* of that fragility and dependence.

Sarton writes that at seventy she has discovered a new power, a power that cohabits with an awareness of powerlessness:

> I am more myself than I have ever been. There is less conflict. I am happier, more balanced, and (I heard myself say rather aggressively) "more powerful." I felt it was rather an odd word, "powerful," but I think it is true. It might have been more accurate to say, "I am better able to use my powers." I am surer of what life is all about, have less self-doubt to conquer.[39]

But then, somewhat ruefully, she admits to the "agony of self-doubt" she had experienced while writing her most recent novel, and later admits to the self-doubt that reappears as she prepares to write her next.

Helen Luke speaks of the task of learning to live *without* the powers we have spent a lifetime building up, "powers which will be taken from us anyway in the fulfilling of the pattern of life and death." (This makes me think of the Sumerian goddess Inanna, who had hoped to go to the Land of No Return girded by all her emblems of power but discovers she must yield them up, one by one, before she may gain admission.)[40] As Luke puts it:

> We may either continue in our last years to cling to our past achievements and worn-out values, thus sinking eventually into complete dependence on others, on collective opinions, demands and attitudes; or we may confront our growing weakness and loss of energy, together with our past rejections, sins and blindness, and so approach that kind of free dependence on "the other" which brings us to the meaning of forgiveness and to kinship with all things.[41]

She sees the power of the old paradoxically to depend on the willingness to accept one's dependence on others and to renounce the will to power, the "will to dominate people or things or our own souls." For if we continue to depend on the ego or the creative spirit to provide us with a sense of meaning and achievement, old age will become nightmare and despair.[42]

Florida Scott-Maxwell, too, affirms the importance of acknowledging that though age is more than a disability, it *is* a disability:

> Being old I am out of step, troubled by my lack of concord, unable to like or understand much that I see. Feeling at variance with the times must be the essence of age, and it is confusing, wounding. I feel exposed, bereft of a right matrix.

She also voices the fear shared by so many older women of the real possibility of suffering a more complete powerlessness, of becoming invalids, of completely losing their independence:

> We wonder how much older we have to become, and what degree of decay we may have to endure. We keep whispering to ourselves, "Is this age yet? How far must I go?" For age can be dreaded more than death. "How many years of vacuity? To

what degree of deterioration must I advance?" . . . Death feels like a friend because it will release us from the deterioration of which we cannot see the end. It is waiting for death that wears us down.

These thoughts are with us always. . . . We are people to whom something important is about to happen.

Where others speak of the Crone's power, Scott-Maxwell speaks of Her *heroic helplessness*. I like that.

She also gives us a sense of the *rage* that may possess the old. Speaking of her life as being "lightly peppered with despair," she confides:

> Disabilities crowd in on the old; real pain is there, and if we have to be falsely cheerful, it is part of our isolation. . . . In silent, hot rebellion we cry silently— "I have lived my life haven't I? What more is expected of me?" Have we got to pretend out of noblesse oblige that age is nothing in order to encourage the others?[43]

Luke spoke of "helpless rage" as one of the gifts of old age, but without the unquestioning approbation of women's anger and rage that sometimes accompanies reflections on the Crone. There *is* valid anger; there *is* creative anger. We are moved by Alcmene in Euripides' *The Children of Heracles* (whose very name means "strong in wrath") powerfully manifesting the energy and aggressiveness of a widow who has rejected the traditional constraints of womanhood. Scott-Maxwell writes of the resurgence of intense feeling that she has experienced as an old woman: "Age puzzles me. I thought it was a quiet time. My seventies were interesting, and fairly serene, but my eighties are passionate. I grow more intense as I age." "I cannot conceive," she muses, "how age and tranquillity ever came to be synonymous."[44]

But not all the anger felt by contemporary old women, or by the old women of mythology, is proportionate, valid, or effective. Luke describes how often the old "remain unaware of underlying despair," yet "sink into a querulous state . . . expressed by projecting all their ills onto circumstances and sometimes onto those on whom they now depend and most need." She notes how often "the ego will endure the worst agonies of neurotic misery rather than consent to the death of even a small part of its demand or its sense of importance." The challenge, as she sees it, is not so much how one responds to "great affliction" but rather how one lives with "the day-by-day onslaughts of hurt feelings, black moods, exhaustion, resentment, and . . . false guilt." The rage becomes "a training ground" for learning the difference between "depression" and "suffering." It is an occasion for learning to see differently, for coming to see that the darkness we project onto others or onto circumstances is our own, yet also for winning freedom from a hubristic guilt about our failures that supposes we *should* have been able to live free of culpability. Ideally, Luke suggests, the old would arrive at a transformed rage which would accept the givenness of their suffering —and yet would still welcome release from it.[45] How much this sounds like Audre Lorde, acknowledging a never eradicated rage at having cancer that begins as primarily a rage at herself ("What had I done wrong and what was I going to have to pay for it and WHY ME?") but which ends with her being able to affirm: "There is nothing I cannot use somehow in my living and my work, even if I would never have chosen it on my own, even if I am livid with fury at having to choose."[46]

Just as the power of the Crone is a strange kind of power, so Her *wisdom* seems to be a strange kind of wisdom, a wisdom permeated with a recognition of how little one knows, and of how apart from that acknowledgment one is really no wiser than one ever was.

The Crone is busily engaged with her *memories*, with telling her story to herself and to all who will listen. The Greeks believed that what occupied the *psyches*, the souls of the dead, in Hades was remembering —not new experience, new thoughts, but simply going over and over the already lived. Remembering becomes re-member-ing, putting the pieces back together to make a new whole. I have listened to my mother going over and over the same vividly recalled events from her years as a child, as a young woman, as middle-aged. Often, from outside, it seems as though no progress is being made, no new insights gained. Often from inside, evidently, it feels as though this remembering is almost a passive experience, happening *to* one. As Scott-Maxwell puts it:

> It amounts to this: that near the end of my life when I am myself as never before, I am awareness at the mercy of multiplicity. Ideas drift in like bright clouds, arresting, momentary, but they come as visitors. A shaft of insight can enter the back of my

mind and when I turn to greet it, it is gone. I did not have it, it had me. My mood is light and dancing, or is leaden. It is not I who choose my moods; I accept them, but from whom?[47]

Yet as I listen to my mother, I know what she is doing is clearly *work* not just passive recall. Many of the memories are painful memories, often somehow apparently more painful when remembered than when lived. She is learning to see them differently, to see herself differently, but the new perspective must be rediscovered over and over again before it is fully absorbed. Luke sees such reevaluating of our past as the point of such remembering: we may discover to our horror how much of what we've done that we were most satisfied with was really done for recognition, comfort, or spiritual merit, how much we thought virtuous or kind really brought harm to others, how in most of our actions there was as much evil as good (though it is still important, she believes, to have aimed at the good).[48] Scott-Maxwell agrees: "One has ample time to face everything one has had, been, done; gather them all in; the things that came from outside, and those from inside. We have time at last to make them truly ours."[49]

As I look at the much-vaunted independence of the Crone, I notice especially how often She is imagined as essentially alone. Sarton and Luke and Scott-Maxwell each seem to see their solitude as deeply informing their capacity to live old age deeply and honestly. Maxwell-Scott, for example, says, "I am so busy being old that I dread interruptions."[50] Elsa Gidlow agrees: "What I needed as I neared my seventieth decade was freedom from commitment to any one individual."[51] I have often wondered how different my mother's experience of being old might be were my father not still alive: would it be easier to move from projecting her rage onto others toward the kind of working-through which the old sometimes achieve without another so readily available to carry the projection? I wonder about this for myself, too. Is there a kind of attending to one's soul that is one of the primary tasks of age which being still centrally engaged in a relationship makes almost impossible? I wonder whether the relationship that presently appears so unquestionably blessed a part of my life will seem so a decade or two or three from now.

While preparing to write this chapter, I had hoped I might have a dream but was denied one. However, something else happened: I lost the ring my partner had given me during our commitment ceremony.

It wasn't loose, had never seemed in any danger of coming off accidentally, but as I sat down to begin my writing I suddenly felt its absence, and we have still not found it. If this had happened in a dream, I might understand it as meaning that the Crone had come to take it away.

As I have sought to attend to what old women have said of their experience of aging, I have come to believe that there is a sense in which no one *is* a crone, in the sense of knowing what it is to be one. As Barbara Macdonald reminds us, even the seventy-year-olds, even those in their eighties and nineties are *discovering* what it's all about. "We are all beginning;"[52] all but initiates in the "rites of ancient ripening" of which Meridel LeSueur sings:

> *Ceremonials of water and fire*
> *Lodge me in the deep, earth*
>   *grind my harvest seed.*
> *The rites of ancient ripening*
> *make my flesh plume*
> *and summer winds stir in my smoked bowl.*[53]

·6·

EVEN THE GODS WILL DIE

I don't believe that my preoccupation with the necessity of coming to terms with change, interdependence, and death bespeaks only a need to confront my own "ripening" and oncoming death. Rather, I see acceptance of transcience and finitude as part of any sustainable celebration of life, as essential to any reconciliation between humankind and the other forms of life with which we share this planet. If this be a crone's "wisdom," so be it. My own understanding of the modes of consciousness which support such acceptance has been immeasurably deepened by my exposure to Egyptian mythology. Here, even more than in the Greek mythology from which I have learned so much, I have been initiated into a perspective which allows me to contemplate the possible death of our species purged of anger or guilt or fearsome denial, imbued instead with an awareness of how intertwined are the destructive energies of our species with our most beautiful and creative powers, how death is a part of all life and how *our* death does not mean the death of all life. Though this truly ancient wisdom is in no way peculiarly a woman's wisdom, I see it communicated most powerfully in a myth about the Egyptian goddess Sekhmet. In this sense, at least, this wisdom, too, begins as a woman's mystery, a wisdom made visible through a female figure.

Poets and Prophets

I woke up one morning remembering nothing of my dream except the long title of a poem: "Love Song To This Doomed Self-Destroying But So Beautifully Creative Species Of Which I Am A Member." If in waking life I were a poet, I would use my gift for words to write this poem; I would compose a love song dedicated to us, to our species, that would celebrate how splendid, how creative, how worthy of honor we have been. I feel so deeply: this poem needs to be written now. As Hölderlin helped us recognize, poems are necessary in times of need:

> . . . *and what use are poets in a time of need?*
> *But, thou sayest, they are like the wine-god's holy priests,*
> *Who go from land to land in the holy night.*[1]

For if we die, if our species and most of the life with which we have shared this planet is destroyed, there will be no one left to mourn, no one left with the capacity to remember us, to say how beautiful we were —no one to write the poem or to hear it.

In a sense the poem would echo themes familiar to me throughout my adult life. I have thought often in recent months of a meeting that took place shortly after the end of World War II with a young man of my own age, a German who had directly experienced those revelations of what human beings can perpetrate and can suffer that my family's escape had protected me from. "How on the other side of all that," I wanted him to tell me, "can one still live as a human being? How can I live my life in a meaningful way?" "By showing that it is still possible to live an ordinary human life, to raise a family in an ordinary way," he said.

The poem I imagine would, I believe, most probably be written by a woman. That there is a female voice, in poetry, in psychology, in theology, is something I both believe and disbelieve. There *is* a perspective different from the dominant one that women in recent years have done much to make audible and to which our experience of our bodies and of oppression may make us especially sensitive—but it is, I believe, a perspective also available to men. My own discovery of this perspective has been intimately connected to my experience of myself as a woman.

I had occasion recently to review an autobiographical essay I'd written while I was in graduate school. It was fascinating to reread this manuscript, to discover the ways in which the young Chris who wrote it is like and unlike the woman I take myself to be today, and moving to see how lovingly and clearly she viewed her familial history and herself. But what struck me most was the section where I wrote, "Perhaps because I am a woman, the issues that seem most important are the ones in which I am personally involved," and then went on to describe how a social vision that began with the concrete demands of family life radiated out to include concerns about racial injustice, nuclear war, the environment, Third World poverty. The paper ended with my saying, "I want my children to understand what I am doing and why."

Then, more than thirty years ago, I was far from any explicit feminist consciousness. But even then I had a sense that my view might be different because it was a woman's view. Since then it has become self-evident to me that women do have easier access to an alternative vision or, at least, that it is easier for women than for men to see through the prevailing vision which is so intricately related to the history of male dominance.

This female perspective is one I might never have discovered on my own, for it is only as women have begun talking about their experience with one another that we have become fully conscious of having been objects not subjects during the long period when male experience was taken as the norm of human experience. Women's talking to one another has taken many forms in the last two decades—informal intimate exchange, consciousness-raising groups, organized classes and symposia, articles and books, art work—but always it has been the sharing of our vulnerability and pain, our confusions, hesitations, and hopes, and our experience of objectification that has enabled us to recognize our distinctive vision.

Having now assumed the subject role, we find it necessary to name what is visible to us *as women*. Our new consciousness allows us to see much which has been more or less hidden—including, I discover, much which, unfortunately, it might be easier not to know—but about which, once seen, one most speak out.

My own awareness has been confirmed and clarified by the testimony of many other women, but recently I find myself particularly indebted to Christa Wolf, the East German novelist, born less than a hundred miles from my birthplace, a year or two earlier than I. I sense a deep affinity with this woman, German but not Jewish, whose life has been so different from mine and yet whose recent writing voices a vision and urgency more closely related to what I feel compelled to say than anything else I know. It helps to have this concern shared.

About ten years ago Christa Wolf published a novel accompanied by four essays in which she examines the figure of the mythic Greek heroine Cassandra—the woman who saw what only a woman would see and was not believed. The epigraph which introduces the essay part of the book comes from Goethe: "This dark race is beyond help; for the most part you have to remain silent so as not to be considered mad like Cassandra, when you prophecy what already lies outside the gate." Through Wolf's representation of Cassandra we are made to participate in the pain of becoming a knowing subject, of seeing too much, of needing to speak out yet not expecting to be heard. Wolf wonders, "Where did Cassandra get the desire and strength to contradict" her compatriots' vision? she asks." "Does there exist an ominous right or duty to bear witness?"[2] Cassandra's prophesying serves as a prototype for Wolf's own writing about the disastrous fate she sees ahead for her own people, us, humankind.

I share Wolf's conviction that if women had had more voice during these last three thousand years, our plight might not be so desperate. Not because we are pure and perfect but because our earliest experiences are ones that foster in us a sense of affiliation and interdependence. As Wolf says, "It is not merely a dreadful, shameful and scandalous fact for women that women were allowed to contribute virtually nothing to the culture we live in, officially and directly, for thousands of years; no, it is strictly speaking the weak point in our culture, which leads to its becoming self-destructive."[3]

But Wolf sees that blame and anger are beside the point, which is not to villainize men but to see better where we are and how we got here, to acknowledge the pain of our separation from the natural world— and the danger—and to recognize that there is no simple going back, no magic reunion.

I, too, must name my fear that we may be moving toward the death of our species and articulate my understanding of what has brought us to this point, though to help with my saying I will rely not on Cassandra but on an image from Egypt. When Troy's doom was sealed, Cassandra fled to the temple of Athene and clung desperately to the goddess's wooden image, hoping for divine protection in a desperate time. Wolf, too, I believe, turns to Athene, the goddess of clear vision and artistic power, to sustain her in this time of need. My own witnessing has most often been inspired by Aphrodite, the goddess of love, but on this occasion her Egyptian counterpart, Hathor (and Hathor's dark other self, Sekhmet) has come to seem even more the figure empowering me to say what I must say—and to say it with love.

Even though I am a feminist and in recent years have chosen to focus my personal love on women, I continue to love men. I believe it is important to take into account the vulnerability and the anxiety that may make otherness so fearful to them and often underlies their focus on achievement and autonomy. I know men as fellow humans and believe that what we are accustomed to calling masculine and feminine perspectives represent complementary not contradictory realities. Indeed, I believe the early experiences of same as *and* separate from the mother available to females may prepare us to view the differences between male and female in a less polarized way. We may not as easily fall into the trap of exaggerating and reifying dissimilarities. We may be able to respond to the differences creatively, to view them as enhancing not diminishing our lives. We might then come to participate in the other's vision as a corollary human possibility—with love and gratitude.

The fears about identity and differentiation so emphatic in male psychology are fears we women also experience, albeit perhaps not as intensely, not as obsessively. In a culture dominated by the male perspective as long as ours has been, women's experience of these fears has inevitably also been amplified. In fact, many of us have discovered to our chagrin how frequently, as women enter traditionally male worlds and take on traditionally male roles, we take on the competitiveness, aggressiveness, impersonal objectivity we have tended to regard as male problems.

These perspectives may be exaggerated among males for whom separation from the mother is more traumatic, but I believe they are integral to our bisexual species, part of *us* not just *them*. The long period of human infantile dependence and our being conscious creatures make the tension between dependence and autonomy, merging and separation almost too much. The contingency of our origin, the known inevitability of our death make our deep ambivalence about both separation and fusion the central problematic of human existence (as Otto Rank saw so clearly).

If we are honest, we need to admit how modern feminism is itself the product of a particular phase of materialist culture. It is no accident that just as our economy needed women to move out of the house, we should all find that we *want* to. Yet I believe the *need* for feminism at this point in our culture is much more far-reaching than that. We are needed now because our view of things is necessary to living this terminal phase in a whole way. I am reminded once again of Freud ending "Analysis Terminable and Interminable" with the observation that the last and most difficult task in an analysis, in an individual life, is integrating the despised feminine aspect, overcoming one's misogyny, one's resistance to the passive or receptive attitude indispensable in so many life situations. Now, I believe, this most difficult task confronts us as a species.

My vision obviously has a tragic dimension, for I see the experience of separation which forms male psychology as an aspect of human experience which we can do little to change. (I have much less confidence than does Dinnerstein or Chodorov that changing our child-rearing practices so as to include fathers in dramatically more equal ways could suffice to avert the catastrophe I foresee.) The conviction that there must be some resolution may be even harder for Americans to surrender than for Europeans. Perhaps it is my European origin that leads me to agree with Wolf that there may be no resolution and that where we find ourselves now may have been determined very far back. "What I ask myself and you," she writes, is:

> Was it necessary that man should come to stand "alone" before Nature—opposite Nature, not in it? . . . Were there crossroads and turning points where humanity—that is European & North American humanity, the inventors and carriers of technological civilization—could have made different decisions, whose resultant course would not have been self-destructive? Was the foundation for future development laid down with the invention of the first weapons for the hunt, with their use against groups competing for food; with the transition from matriarchally structured, less effective groups, to patriarchal, economically more effective ones? When proportions still commensurate with human experience were exceeded?
> Or was it laid down from the beginning?[4]

The question is one I, too, cannot answer with any certainty, although like Wolf I suspect it may have been laid down from the beginning. As Eugenio Montale also seems to suggest in his poem "Brooding":

> *Probably*
> *evening is falling. . . .*
> . . . .
> *If it becomes clear the First Causes*
> *already contained the explosion of the ridiculous*
> *   then we'll have to look elsewhere, though*
> *without success*
> *since the future already passed some time ago.*[5]

I am no Cassandra; my question is a subtly and yet significantly different one from Wolf's. What I ask myself and you is: If it *was* laid down from the beginning, how can we most wholly live this end time which has been bequeathed to us?

I would want to emphasize what Wolf only intimates: that the very values which are self-destructive are also beautiful—worthy of our respect, our love and mourning, as those who have lived by them and who may also be destroyed by them are worthy of our compassion and honor. I have a profound conviction that it is what is most beautiful in us humans, what is most distinctive about our species, that may destroy us. Not something evil or accidental and eradicable but rather something inherent in that combination of consciousness and finitude which characterizes human being—our longing to understand, to make, to transform, to perpetuate. It seems nearly inevitable that we should have believed ourselves transcendent to nature—and then have had to rediscover our continued subservience to her.

I do not look to a return to nature or to the early stages of human history as possible or desirable. As Wolf says, the motto Know Thyself could not have occurred to any goddess in the undifferentiated age. On the other hand it is also true that the equation of the feminine and the natural is a product of simplistic dichotomous thinking. It seems likely that women *began* culture, agriculture, though that discovery was probably understood as a participation in natural processes rather than as an abrogation of them.

The pulls toward differentiated knowledge, toward rationality, toward mastery, toward autonomy are precious—which, because they have for these many millennia not been balanced by the equally precious pulls toward intimacy, toward the concrete, toward acceptance of the given, may do us in. As Dinnerstein puts it, we now face the challenge of learning to reconcile our wish for "I"ness with "our wish to survive as a species and the wish to enjoy the color, taste, texture and smell of our short individual lives."[6]

That women now have a voice again cannot, I believe, change what has happened—but it may enable us to live differently what is still to happen . It may enable us to face together that we human beings may, indeed, bring about an end to the life of our species and to most of the other life on this beautiful planet that has been our home. Perhaps through the bomb, perhaps through some more gradual irreparable transformation of the environment on which life depends. Perhaps not immediately, perhaps not even in our children's time, but very likely sometime, very likely too soon.

That is painfully sad, but to me it is even sadder that we put all our energies into denying the possibility or into trying to avert or at least delay its realization. I value those valiant efforts to avert, but fear that they, too, serve as a kind of denial which may inhibit us from attending to another task: honoring who we have been and grieving that we may soon not be. And I wonder if our focus on averting may still not participate in the hubris that brought us here to begin with, the hubris of thinking we can know enough to comprehend the whole. As was true of Oedipus, what we do to avoid our fate often just seems to make it more inevitable.

Let me make clear that I, too, know the superstitious fear that imagining brings it on, that Cassandra is responsible for Troy's doom. I, too, often feel that I can only bear to believe it might all end if I can also believe that, if we only respond rightly, it won't. But as a postmenopausal woman I have found that the most important personal life task I now confront is learning how to die well (that is, how to live well in the face of my oncoming death). I have also come to see that the most important service I can now render to humankind may be encouraging us to think together about what dying well as a species might mean. I see us in a situation analogous to that of an individual suffering a terminal disease. We *can* put all our energies into looking for every possible remedy or delay, so busy averting that we leave no time for celebrating what has been, mourning what will not be, or saying farewell. Some would choose that as the most courageous response; it would not be my choice.

To move, even now, to a different understanding of the relation between the human and the natural world might help us toward a different response—toward an acceptance of the finitude not just of the individual human but of our species, toward a realization that we are not in control, do not ultimately have dominion over nature after all, and that we will end.

Just as we have for so long identified the human with the male, so we have seen the divine only in human terms, thereby disavowing our dependence on nature. It is deeply moving that we take ourselves so seriously, love our form of life so much, that we can see the divine only in this image. But this means that if we die, the gods, the divine, die with us—which somehow (at least for me) makes our probable death even more unbearable.

Beginning at the Beginning

I had the dream of writing the love poem to our species shortly after a visit to Nagasaki with my daughter. Earlier that same year I had been in

Egypt. The exposure in Egypt to a consciousness so ancient that even the Greeks were awed at its age has played an important part in my own working through toward a reconciliation with the possibility that we may really die as a species.

I first went to Egypt at the time of the winter solstice, the time of the year's beginning, and felt myself to be at the place of beginnings. I have been to Delphi and felt the presence of the divine there, understood fully why the Greeks knew it as the navel of the world, but to be at Karnak at dawn in midwinter and to watch the sun rise perfectly centered between that long line of gates is another order of experience. There I knew myself to be at the place where humans first left enduring and immediately comprehensible evidence of their response to the divine—evidence that still has the power to move and teach me. I remembered my own early fascination with Egypt, older even than my father-taught love of Greece, and my childhood dream of going there and beginning at the beginning.

I know that Egypt is not literally the beginning, but it seems to be where I have to begin now. The goddesses of ancient Egypt have stirred a level of my being not touched by the gods of the Greeks or even by their goddesses. The Greeks said that Tartarus lies as far below the surface of the earth as earth lies below Olympus. Similarly, in my soul, what Egypt touches seems to lie as far below what the goddesses (except perhaps Gaia) touch in me as that lies below what is touched by the gods. Of course I am aware how relatively near to us dynastic Egypt is compared to the Old European cultures Marija Gimbutas has so powerfully brought to life and which have inspired the work of so many other feminist scholars. They focus on the period between 6500 B.C.E. and 3500 B.C.E., which leaves off just about where I am now pulled to begin. Perhaps an engagement with the truly archaic prehistorical past may still await me, but I know that what I need to do now is to turn toward the beginning of history, of that past available to us through written sources, that past which has directly shaped our present. Gimbutas herself acknowledges how data from this later period "supplements and verifies our understanding of the appearance and functions of the prehistoric goddess. Written sources pour blood into her veins of stone, clay, bone or gold."[7]

My need to move toward the past, stage by stage, from the goddesses of classical Greece to Gaia, and now to Egypt, reminds me of the dream that Jung had while sailing to America with Freud, the dream which revealed to him the existence of a collective dimension to the psyche more primordial than the personal unconscious on which he saw Freud focusing. In the dream he found himself moving downward from the richly furnished rococo upper story of "his house" to the medieval-feeling ground floor and then down a stone staircase to a beautifully vaulted Roman cellar; still farther below he found a low rock-faced cave whose floor was covered with scattered bones and broken bits of primitive pottery. This cave, he came to believe, represented a primitive aspect of the psyche scarcely reachable by consciousness.[8]

I envy Gimbutas her gift for apprehending the meaning of such bones and fragments. She sees, and helps me to see, patterns and connections invisible to most of us. She reads the symbolic content of such patterns and can then move on to infer the beliefs, the myths and rituals, that inspired their creation. She seems able imaginatively to recreate the human lives of the makers. Compared to her grasp of Old Europe, my understanding of the Egyptian world, despite its being so much closer to us, is still fragmentary and provisional, and will always be dependent on the scholarship of others.

I cannot go to an ancient site and dig for the buried vestiges of a classical civilization. I cannot even, without assistance, interpret the relics, the temples, the reliefs or sculptures that others have uncovered. Still, I know that my understanding and appreciation of old Egypt have been immeasurably deepened by having been there. I know, too, that after turning to books and museums to help me understand what I saw, I want to return—to the Nile, to Sakkara, to Luxor, and, above all, to Abydos.

Even the little I already know persuades me how much we might learn from ancient Egypt. I was, of course, at first particularly interested in the goddesses and had expected these divine figures would complement, expand, and perhaps challenge that understanding of feminine possibilities I had garnered from the years devoted to study of the goddesses of Greece. Now I am less sure that what *these* goddesses teach is still psychology or that it is about the feminine in any immediately human sense. To begin to understand anything of the Egyptian goddesses, I discovered that I had first to apprehend how wholly different Egyptian mythological consciousness is from that of Greece. Now, looking back on what I have learned, I believe the initiation into this consciousness—which teaches a different relationship to our bodies, to our species, to our planet, to death and to endings—has itself been the most valuable gift.

I found that the goddesses of ancient Egypt initiated me into very different modes of awareness from those associated with the Greek goddesses with whom I was so much more familiar, although the Greeks themselves seem not to have recognized the profundity of the difference. Herodotus and other early Greek visitors to Egypt were awed by the ancientness of her mythology and the alienness of its manifestations—the multiplicity of divinities, the barbarism of the composite animal-human forms. Although their initial response was antipathy and bewilderment, they believed that their own divinities were of universal validity, were archetypes, eternally valid realities, and so they assumed that the Egyptian divinities were essentially the same as their own but with different names. They equated Isis with Demeter, Hathor with Aphrodite, Nut with Rhea, Neith with Athene.

Yet I believe this is to miss the point. It is what is unique and distinctive In the Eqyptian apprehension that speaks to me. I again recall Rilke's passionate plea: "Let none of the gods vanish. We need each and every one. Every one should matter to us, every perfected image."9 Thus I believe that we should aim at making visible the peculiar essence of the Egyptian perspective, rather than imposing on it our criteria of rationality (as the Greeks seem to have done and as many nineteenth-century Egyptologists did) and therefore dismissing it, or interpreting it in evolutionary terms (as Breasted did early in this century) and thus overemphasizing those features which can be read as prefiguring ethical monotheistic religiosity.

Thanks to its relative isolation, Egypt provides us with a unique opportunity to study a culture in which the transition from the archaic to the dynastic period proceeds as an essentially internal development. For predynastic Egypt we must rely on the same kinds of nonliterary visual sources which Gimbutas uses to decipher the cultures of Old Europe; such data suggest many similarities between the early period in Egypt and in the rest of the Mediterranean world. (Someday I hope also to learn more about the connections between Egypt and other early African cultures.)

Suddenly around 3200 B.C.E., without anything comparable to the Indo-European invasion, a highly complex large-scale civilization appeared. A single monarch ruled from the Delta to Nubia; the "Two Lands," North and South, were unified. Writing was introduced (perhaps from Mesopotamia); the potter's wheel, masonry, a calendar made their appearance. Although there is, undoubtedly, some influence from

Mesopotamia, the western Mediterranean, from Libya and Africa, there was no disruption.

What we know of the prehistorical mythology is slight. The Egyptian word for the divine, *ntr*, probably initially referred to the standards from which banners depicting animal images were flown at the entrances to ancient temples and carried in ritual processions. Among the animal forms depicted on such standards at a very early period were the baboon, the ibis, and the jackal, forerunners of such later divinities as Thoth and Anubis. Although there is no certain evidence for any anthropomorphic divinity in predynastic Egypt, there were theriomorphic precursors of the later female and male gods. Probably the first living creature worshiped throughout Egypt was the hawk, already known as Horus (and as incarnate in the pharoah) by the time of the first dynasty.

Gimbutas might be able to confirm that the many clay and ivory figurines of humanlike females dating back to the Naqada period are, indeed, representations of a mother goddess; the evident absence of any images of nude goddesses in the early historical period leads the male scholars I have read to find this interpretation questionable. There does seem to be agreement that in Egypt, as in Gimbutas's Old Europe, the oldest female divinities were not earth-mother goddesses but goddesses of the air. The earliest home of the gods was the sky; the most ancient goddess was Hathor, whose name depicts her as the deified House of Horus, that part of the sky through which the hawk flies. In the prehistoric period the sky was already represented as a cow which gave birth each day to a calf, the bull of heaven. In dynastic Egypt the earth was envisioned as a male divinity, Geb, while the sky remained a female domain. In Egypt, where the life-bringing water comes from the Nile not from the sky, the sky cow's udders were not seen as source of the nurturing rain as they often were in Old Europe.

Echoing the Old Europe pattern are Egypt's very ancient bird and serpent goddesses; later these divinities often appear in the hybrid animal-human form so characteristic of dynastic Egyptian iconography. The persistence of the ancient deities into the historical period means that there are names and sometimes tales associated with the visual images, though the etymological significance of the names may be entirely obscure and the known tales may be very late.

The vulture goddess who came to be regarded as the protective deity of Upper Egypt was called Nekhebet; the official protectress of the North was the serpent goddess Buto, often represented as a winged cobra. Both were also seen as having a destructive aspect: the vulture devouring the dead as carrion; the serpent destroying with her venomous spit. An ancient goddess of the Theban necropolis, Merseger, was represented as a human-headed snake; Renenet, a birth goddess, appeared as a woman with the head of a cobra. The bird goddesses were seen as life restoring; their flapping wings waft breath into the nostrils of the deceased. The archaic wide-winged vulture eventually became wing-enfolding Isis. The snake goddesses represented cosmic order, the necessary complementary relation between birth and death. In the dynastic period they appear most significantly as the uraeus, the symbol of divine and royal power. This venomous sun-encircling cobra was identified with the Eye of Re and thus with Sekhmet, the goddess whom I have come to find my most challenging teacher.

In predynastic Egypt there were other counterparts to the goddesses of Old Europe: Heket, a water goddess in the form of a frog, who was associated with childbirth and with the newly germinating grain, and Taueret, a protectress of women in pregnancy and childbirth, who was represented as a pregnant hippopotamus with human breasts and the hind legs of a lioness. However, as far as I know, the bees and butterflies so important elsewhere do not enter into Egyptian mythological tradition.

The earliest cults focused on these animal gods, but other aspects of the natural world were also felt to be divine: water (especially, of course, the river on which life in Egypt so clearly depends), the earth, the sun. The oldest creation myth begins with the primeval watery abyss out of which emerges a scarab. Pushing at the mud, the beetle forms the primeval earth hill, as each year the fertile land emerges from the receding Nile. There are few specific traditions about the origin of human beings; our creation is generally implicitly subsumed as part of the creation of all living things (usually accredited to the sun).

In Egypt earth and sun were male, as was the moon which was associated with Thoth, the mathematician, messenger, and magician, and with shaven-headed Khonsu. The moon is Re's placenta, his afterbirth, or the weaker, left eye of Horus. I have found no evidence pointing to a moon goddess.

That human-shaped gods appeared for the first time along with the monarchy is confirmed by the fact that the earliest pharoahs all bore animal names, whereas after the second dynasty none do. Unification of the kingdom also required some unification of the local religious traditions, although it is known that each village continued to have its own protective divinity, often a female deity, throughout the pharonic period, and it is likely that the cult of several of the older divinities was already widespread prehistorically. The nationally most important gods were distinguished by being represented seated on thrones and carrying the emblems of life and power. After writing was introduced, these gods were brought into relationship with one another through the genealogical systems created by the priests associated with the major cult centers, though there was never one established authoritative pantheon.

The central, most highly elaborated historical myth, the one involving Osiris, Isis, and Horus, may have been created to stabilize monarchical succession, though the divinities involved all have antecedents in the predynastic period when their primary association was with natural phenomena. Horus and Isis were bird gods; Osiris was god of the Nile and of the grain which grows from the inundated soil. Set, who appears in the myth linked to the accession ritual as Osiris's murderous, usurping brother, was originally identified with the desert which threatens and destroys Osiris's vegetation. Through an easily comprehensible process Set also became associated with night and death, the necessary complements, the requisite interludes.

The later priests and kings (long before Ahkenaten) tried to impose a solar-focused (though not monotheistic) spirituality on Egypt, but the sun seems to have played a more important role in theological speculation than in cult. Osiris was always a more popular deity than Re or Atum or Amun—perhaps the unknown source of the Nile felt more mysterious than the course of the sun, perhaps in his most common representation as a mummiform human he seemed more intimately available to humankind. Even Re, the oldest sun god, was (Budge believes)[10] felt to be an Asiatic import; worship of the scarab (which is later viewed as a manifestation of Re) is clearly much older than worship of Re. Atum, the solar god who creates parthenogenetically by masturbating, was probably created in a relatively late period, as part of a rationalizing synthesis proposed by the Heliopolis priests. The speculative origin of this god is implied by his name, which means "the one who has been completed by absorbing others"; the lateness, by his always appearing with a human head. Amun, also, is a late-appearing divinity, although he is retrospectively represented as an early god. His name refers to his hiddenness, his invisibility and inscrutability. Even the myths show him as an intruder at most shrines.

EVEN THE GODS WILL DIE · 163

Although there are evident changes in Egyptian religiosity correlative with the beginning of the monarchy and the introduction of writing, we need to remember how early this transition is—more than two millennia earlier than Homer. We must also take account of how very different our sources of knowledge about Egyptian divinities are from the sources we rely on for our understanding of Greek deities. For Egypt we are dependent on the evidence provided by temples, tombs, reliefs, statues, on the inscriptions accompanying many of these monuments and on ritual texts. Although there are many written allusions to familiar myths, there are no full narrations of them, no shaped literary versions of the mythology like those provided by Homer and Hesiod. Indeed, the only fully rendered Egyptian myth available to us from the ancient world is Plutarch's late retelling of the Osiris tradition.

The absence of a literary tradition (which means that Egyptian mythology was never subject to the esthetic concern for shaping, defining, simplifying) may help explain its immediately evident fluidity. I see Egyptian mythology as therefore closer to the mythic as opposed to the esthetic imagination, closer to primary process, closer to the logic of dreams than to the logic of waking life. It seems to give expression to a logic to which we still have access but which we tend not to trust. Thus Egypt fascinates—and repels.

The same natural phenomenon, for instance, the sun, can in Egypt be seen in relation to several themes, to creation, rebirth, and justice. The same subject, death, may be understood by reference to many phenomena, to the serpent and the lion, to the sun, the stars, the grain. The same divinity may be manifest in a variety of forms; as Nut, for example, is cow, sky, roof, woman, a heavenly body of water. The same animal may be the manifestation of several different divinities; as the cow may be Nut or Hathor or Isis.

The fluidity and apparent confusion resist interpretation. I remember Sartre saying of existential psychology, "This psychoanalysis has not yet found its Freud." Of Egypt I would say, "This mythology has not yet found its Otto." No one has yet succeeded in writing about the Egyptian deities and communicating (as Walter Otto did for the Greek gods and goddesses) the source of their power to move humans to worship over many millennia. We have not really understood that the Egyptians did not invent these realities but experienced them as providing satisfying answers to their deepest questions and longings. Although empathic understanding of Egyptian mythology seems to require a much more demanding relinquishment of our accustomed values and thought habits than is called for in entering into Greek consciousness, the effort promises to teach us more we do not already know. Perhaps an inner appropriation of Egyptian mythological consciousness could help us recognize the dangers of one-sided reliance on linear, abstract, antithetical thinking not simply to our individual psychic balance but to the very survival of life on this planet.

Among the most distinctive and most often misunderstood features of Egyptian consciousness is the delight in multiplicity and multiplication. We soon discover that there was no fixed, final form associated with any major divinity. To the ancient Egyptians changelessness meant death, nonexistence, whereas we have tended to impose on them a Platonic valuation of the unchanging and eternal and thus to misapprehend their notion of long-lastingness. We fail to see that for them creation meant differentiation; life meant change. Their deities were alive, and thus still in process like their temples to which additions were always still being made. (At Karnak the construction process went on for millennia, with pharoahs continually adding new halls and pylons to the Amun temple and building shrines to other divinities alongside it, often reusing stones first brought to the site by far-distant predecessors.)

To the Egyptians singularity, oneness, signified nonexistence. Life begins with creative differentiation, with duality. Dualistic thinking (perhaps originally inspired by the extreme contrast between the fertile jungle at the Nile's edge and the harsh desert just beyond) figures prominently in Egyptian mythology. It is the task of the goddess of justice, Maat, to keep the antitheses, desert and river, chaos and order, in balance. Because a unity was conceived as the integration of two complementary realities, they always spoke of their land as "the Two Lands." Egypt was created by the joining of the south with its narrow strip of inhabitable land to the so obviously different wide Delta region in the north. In the ancient traditions the divine was most often represented as appearing in male/female pairs with balanced powers (though not too surprisingly in the dynastic period there was much less official emphasis on the goddesses—who came to be relegated to wifely and other supportive and subordinate roles).

Perhaps most strangely to us, even nonexistence was perceived as a reality complementary to existence and as divine: Shu, the empty space between earth and sky; Set, the empty desert. Set is especially interesting. The myths represent him as the necessary opponent of Re, Osiris,

Horus, and as the good loser. Because death is a necessary interlude, the essential prelude to regeneration, Set is a helper of the dead.

Egyptian duality, however, is but the most simple form of plurality; the logic of Egyptian mythology is not primarily antithetical but plurivocal. The mythology develops, not in the direction of monotheism or philosophy, but rather in the direction of an ever more complex polytheism. The both/and additive logic does not mean that the Egyptians were muddled in their thinking, but simply that their assumptions were radically different from those of Hellenic logic. The Egyptian approach reminds me of Jung's interpretive method, which proceeds by way of amplification rather than reduction. As Hathor is cow and hippopotamus and sycamore tree and lioness, so the male figure in my dream is brother and therapist and Hermes and the alchemical bridegroom. The Egyptians stressed the complementation rather than the incompatibility of alternative views. Tolerant and flexible, they were ever ready to change and expand their religious conceptions but unwilling to abandon earlier versions—a conservatism Freud taught us to recognize as characteristic of primary process consciousness.

When the Egyptians apprehended an analogy between two divinities, these divinities were seen as combined into one. The process was one of assimilation not repression. Re and Amon were both sun gods —they did not supplant one another, neither was the real one, but when they met, a third being, Re-Amon, was created. Re and Osiris were daily unified. Re became Re-Osiris as the sun set and entered Osiris's underworld realm. Each morning Osiris unsuccessfully struggled with Re to rise with him and like him become a heavenly god, but each day they separated. There were clear limitations on the identification between deities; each retained his or her identity. The priest had to declare to whichever god he addressed: "I have not equated your nature with that of another god."[11] Isis and Hathor were often combined as were Mut and Sekhmet, Sekhmet and Bast, Sekhmet and Hathor—but as in dreams, only temporarily. The union could be dissolved, the separate divinities continued to persist. The composite form was a distinct creature.

Thus Egyptian mythology expresses a delight in polytheism, variety, differentiation and an apparent immunity to the pull toward monotheism, abstraction, and unification. Image and thought were irreducibly united. The Egyptians used the elements of the natural world— sun, earth, sky, air, and water—to think toward intuitive answers for their questions about origin, justice, survival, meaning. The universe was alive; the divine was immanent in the natural world. This immanence facilitated recognition of the correlations between human and natural life. The narrowness of the band of fertile land forced them to live very close to the river and to the animals who also gathered by it. The inescapable intimate contact made their awareness of their relation to nature a matter of direct experience not an intellectual conclusion. The Egyptians seem not to have had a sense of the divine apart from its particular manifestations. The world before creation was a world without gods. *Ntr* always appears only in conjunction with a deity's name, never as an abstraction.

The immanent, concrete focus of the Egyptian imagination meant that they also did not conceive of the survival of a soul apart from some physical substratum, which might be the mummified body but could also be some other tangible representation, a sculpture or a painting. From our perspective their way of conjoining the permanent and the changing may easily seem strange. What they imitate in stone are the perishable artifacts of their everyday existence; the models for their enormous granite pillars are living forms like the papyrus plant and the lotus.

We may easily misjudge the Egyptian attitude toward death because its monuments have survived, whereas little of the material evidence of their everyday existence has. Thus we may read morbidity and fear in what appears like an obsession with death and may not perceive that it is precisely because they so delighted in life here that they sought to perpetuate it. The longing for continued life was not a longing for fixity. The Egyptians did not imagine that the individual soul persists eternally in some one new form, nor even that there was a linear series of forms through which it might pass.

The Egyptian vision of an afterlife was not a belief in metempsychosis, in the transmigration of souls. There was no conception of some permanent inhabitation of another life form. There was not even the notion of a single enduring soul. The deceased were buried on the west, the sunset, side of the Nile, so that they might join Osiris in the underworld. The successful passage of the various trials and challenges they confronted was not really morally determined but rather dependent on ritual and magic, particularly on having undertaken the Abydos pilgrimage during one's lifetime. The goal was to become Osiris. Nevertheless, following the same path as the sun, they would also move into the heavens; there, as *Akhu*, they would persist in the sphere of the changeless, the totally withdrawn realm of the stars. Yet they might also appear to the living in their *ba* form, just as Osiris appears in the form of his *ba,* the phoenix.

The gods were said to be at home in the world of the dead and to emerge from it only on specific occasions. (The essential invisibility of the gods was acknowledged by keeping the cultic statues which repre-sented them hidden in the dark inner sanctuaries which only the priests might enter and keeping them veiled even when they were carried about during a ritual procession.) But actually there is no land of the dead per se—just the natural world. Thus *we* might seek to describe the Egyptian hopes concerning an afterlife by saying they looked forward to participating in the ongoing life of the natural universe. But, of course, *they* never put it so abstractly. They spoke rather of becoming Osiris, and thus of becoming the vegetal growth, the rising Nile, the rising sun. One of their most beautiful images shows Osiris wrapped like a human mummy, lying on his side, with grain stalks growing from his body.

Beyond the Anthropomorphic

We, as Denise Levertov sees, are only "beginners" at recovering a relation to the natural world which those who were there at the begin-ning took for granted:

> *But we have only begun*
> *to love the earth.*
>
> *We have only begun*
> *to imagine the fullness of life.*
> . . . .
>
> *how it might be*
> *to live as siblings with beast and flower not as*
> *oppressors.*
>
> *Surely our river*
> *cannot already be hastening*
> *into the sea of nonbeing?*

Surely it cannot
drag, in the silt,
all that is innocent?

Not yet, not yet—

. . . . . .

So much is unfolding that must
complete its gesture,

so much is in bud. [12]

In Egypt the recognition of the sacredness of the natural world, including its animal inhabitants, was not characteristic only of some early, later discarded, animistic phase; it persisted long after the introduction of anthropomorphic deities. The divine was seen as present not just in art, ritual, or myth but in living beings, in particular animals, and in the reigning pharoah.

Even in its most mature phase their religion still communicated that recognition of the power of the natural world as greater than human power which first inspired it. When anthropomorphic gods appeared, perhaps during the First Dynasty when the balance between animal and human may have been felt to have shifted and when the function of religion became more clearly political, the new forms were added to the already present ones, not understood as replacements of them. The mixed forms, the hybrid animal-human gods, introduced during the second or third dynasty were also seen as supplementary representations.

The hybrid forms (which the later Greek visitors to Egypt found so barbaric and repellent) were common in Old Europe and may have been brought to Egypt from Mesopotamia. Elsewhere they disappear after the Indo-European invasions; in Egypt they persist. Obviously the Egyptians did not believe that there *are* such creatures but used these hybrid representations to express their sense of the simultaneous presence in a divinity of complementary attributes and powers. The same divinity could be represented in animal form, in hybrid form, in human form; the same term, *neteru*, was applied to all these forms of divinity. Hathor might be a cow giving suck to a pharoah, a human with a cow face, or a beautiful human female. No one of these forms is felt to be a truer representation. Nor was there any development among the

Egyptians toward a purely anthropomorphic nor an abstract conception of divinity; the images were seen as the most telling representation.

The gods were seen as *in* the animals or other aspects of the natural world with which they were associated but not identical with them. For example (except in the Akhenaten period), the word for sun was different from the the name of the sun god. The god inhabited or resided in the animal but this incarnation did not define the god. Thoth was present in the moon as well as in the baboon and also in the ibis. None of these was a privileged representation nor is there any implication that moon, baboon, and ibis were therefore somehow profoundly alike. Thoth was in each precisely because none fully communicate all that he is; the god could be present in more than one place at a time. The god might be identified with one particular representative of an animal species—as the Apis bull in Memphis *is* Ptah—or with the species as such. The divinity of the animal was not just an allegory; the divine was actually felt to be present *here*. But not everywhere. There was no development in the direction of pantheism. Not everything was divine. That also would for the Egyptians be too abstract a conception.

The Egyptians' apprehension of the natural world was in no sense sentimental. The animals they worshiped were often fearful and destructive, like the lion, the hippopotamus, the crocodile, and the scorpion. Their sense of the divinity inherent in animal life cannot be reduced to terror or to the recognition of dependency. Animals represented a mysterious nonhuman, and thus superhuman, mode of being, a radical otherness. As in Rilke's Eighth Elegy, animals were seen as living in the present as we do not and so as free of death:

> *All other creatures look into the Open,*
> *with their whole eyes. But our eyes,*
> *turned inward, are all set around like snares,*
> *trapping its way out to freedom.*
>
> . . . .
>
> *. . . the free animal*
> *always has its destruction behind*
> *and god ahead, and when it moves,*
> *it moves toward eternity like running springs.* [13]

In the Egyptian view each member of a species in a sense *is* the species. Animals are seen as not subject to the concern with individuality that plagues humankind. I find it striking that among the Egyptians the only thing that was never perceived as divine is the living human individual. There were no mythological heroes. The pharoah was divine as Horus, in his representative role not in his individual existence, and was not worshiped during his lifetime (though statues of him were). During his human life the gods were his parents; after his death they became his siblings.

In Egypt even the gods will die. Eternity and existence were experienced as contradictions. The scale of the gods' lifespan is of a different order from ours but not endless. "Decay and disappearance await every god, every goddess, all animals, and all insects."[14] Infinity, like singularity, meant death, nonexistence. The gods were finite and corporeal; they are born, grow old and tired and impotent, and they die. Osiris was murdered, dismembered and buried. Re was weary and aged at the end of every day and nightly met his corpse. As the eons pass, the daily renewal became too much for him. He abdicated and allowed Nut to carry him on her generous back and convey him to the furthest sky. Thoth, the god of measure, assigned a fixed lifetime to each of the gods.

Texts of all periods, the Coffin Texts and the Book of the Dead, refer to a final, definitive end to the time of the gods. After "millions of years," Atum says, "This earth will return to the primeval water, to endless flood as in its first state. I shall remain with Osiris after I have transformed myself into another snake which men do not know and the gods do not see." That is, Atum will become Apopis, the snake who is the eternal enemy of the gods, who represents chaos and formlessness. The state of things before creation will return. Another text puts it even more radically: "There is no god, there is no goddess, who will make himself, who will make herself, into another snake."[15]

I see Egypt as introducing us to a consciousness which loves life but does not fear death, which finds divinity in the manifest, the palpable and the embodied, and which celebrates variety, plurality, and change. The ancient Egyptians were humble and reverent before the natural world and longed to belong to it more fully than our fetishistic attachment to our individuality and humanity easily allows.

Egyptian Goddesses

My initiation into this consciousness has been conducted in large measure by the goddesses of ancient Egypt, particularly by Isis, Hathor, and

Sekhmet. I have learned much from these figures, though not what I expected. I do not experience them as models for my own struggles, as representations of aspects of my own psyche, nor as personal presences. The Egyptian goddesses are creatrices; they have created us humans, along with all natural life. They nurture us. They welcome us at death.

But neither in myth or cult was there any personal relationship between these goddesses and individual humans —nothing comparable to the bonds between Athene and Odysseus, Aphrodite and Helen, or between Zeus and one of his mortal mistresses, and little personal piety until the state disintegrates. The human relation to the divine is mediated through the natural world and the pharoah.

Gimbutas asks, what happened to the prehistoric Old Europe goddess after the third millennium and the advent of patriarchal Indo-European culture? Did she survive the dramatic change? In Egypt where there was no such traumatic intervention, the goddesses survived with less alteration. They remained closer to the natural world; they became less individualized.

Echoes of an original connection between the Greek goddesses and aspects of nature persist in the classical period—Artemis was shown accompanied by two does; Aphrodite inspired the lovemaking of wolves and panthers, not only of humans; Hera was often described as cow-eyed—but, in the post-Homeric world, these goddesses were clearly humanlike albeit immortal beings. It was precisely their emancipation from the natural that made them divine. As Nietzsche observed, the Greek gods "justified human life by living it—the only satisfactory theodicy ever invented."[16] The Egyptian goddesses, on the other hand, were still intimately identified with the natural world; their divinity resided in their not being human.

Immanence is correlated with impersonality. The Egyptian goddesses were not distinct individuals as their Greek counterparts were; they are not human females writ large. They differed from one another not in character but rather in function and sphere of action, which is why they so easily combined and then separated. They provided no specific assistance, issued no divine commands. The Egyptians saw us as living our human lives dependent on the right performance of ritual and on the exercise of our human wisdom.

The goddesses were numerous. Each village had its own and often the principal regional deity was female, a local goddess who might from time to time be paired with one of the great national gods or on occasion identified with one or another of the national goddesses. A great variety of wild and domestic animals were worshiped as feminine deities, including cats, lions, vultures, cobras, scorpions, crocodiles, hippopotamuses, and cows. Powerful female divinities were included among each of the nationally significant pantheons, the Heliopolitan, the Memphite, the Hermopolitan, the Theban.

Goddesses were more important in early tradition and continuingly in popular religious life than modern scholars or the official Egyptian theologies themselves usually recognize. Naturally the monarchical and national priestly traditions emphasized the gods associated with validating the patriarchally organized government, the gods the pharoah incarnated and worshiped. (Though the subliminal importance of the goddesses is still evident: the pharoah proclaims himself to be "the Two Ladies," to have incorporated into his being the vulture goddess who represented Upper Egypt and the serpent goddess who represented the North.) Modern scholars have followed suit; there have been no focused extended studies devoted to a particular Egyptian goddess (except for several books about the worship of Isis in the Graeco-Roman period—an Isis who is clearly more a Hellenistic divinity than a truly Egyptian one).

The best-known Egyptian creation myths focused on the activity of male gods. As in Old Europe the primal element out of which all life emerged was water. Re created himself by rising from the primeval waters enclosed in a lotus bud, or he first appeared as a rising phoenix. Each morning he was born as a calf on the western horizon. He gave birth out of his own body to the first divine couple; all life came from his sweat and tears. Atum created himself, as by an act of will or utterance he arose in serpent form from the watery abyss. He then created the rest of the living world by masturbating, spitting, and vomiting. Thoth, also self-begotten, opened his lips upon first stirring himself to consciousness; the sound materialized as the original four gods and four goddesses. In his ibis form he hatched the world egg. (This act is also attributed to Geb, the cackling Nile goose.) Ptah created by speaking or by the exercise of his magic artistry. Khnum created on a potter's wheel; all that lives was formed of sun-baked Nile mud. (It was told that he fashioned the body and *ka* of the female pharoah, Hatshepsut, and implanted them in her mother's womb.) There was no attempt to reconcile these various accounts. The gods and goddesses created one another. Re was father of his father. Horus was born of Isis before Isis comes into being.

There were, however, more ancient traditions, which recognized the creative role of goddesses. One of the oldest Egyptian divinities was Neith. Already widely worshiped in the predynastic period, she was later absorbed into the Osiris cult and became even more important in the Late Period when there was a deliberate return to archaic traditions in the hope that this might encourage political stability. Both mother and daughter of Re, she was the primeval watery mass, the first parthenogenetically creative being. She was judge and sorceress. As goddess of the battle and of the hunt, she carried two arrows and a shield. She was also the weaver who prepared the linen clothing worn by the dead.

Nut was goddess of the sky, the home of the gods. Her elongated body was arched over the earth, with fingertips and toes barely touching. Each trembling limb was supported by two gods; her belly by another. Though daughter to Re, she was also his mother for she gave birth to him every day. Each evening he was swallowed up by her mouth; at dawn he emerged from her vagina. Each morning she ate her children, the stars, as a sow eats her piglets. The hieroglyph by which she is identified depicts a womb. A goddess associated with childbirth and fertility, Nut was represented as a hippopotamus and sometimes as a cow wearing Hathor's horns and disk. Like the Greek Gaia, she embodied a fertile procreativity which on occasion was terrifying to males. One myth tells of how when she was pregnant with her twin brother Geb's children, Re decreed that she might not give birth during any month of the year. Luckily, in a game of draughts with the moon the inventive Thoth wins for her the five intercalary days during which she is able to deliver Osiris, Seth, Isis, Nepthys, and the Elder Horus. To my mind the most beautiful image associated with this goddess is the one that recognizes in the goddess of birth the goddess of rebirth, and depicts her on the inner lid of a sarcophagus as a lovely woman in a star-studded gown with arms outstreched above her head. Her full-bodied embrace welcomes us when we die; in death we will take our place among the stars in the sky.

Isis, too, was originally far more than the devoted wife and mother she became in the later strata of the traditions. Somehow in the process of absorbing the functions and attributes of all the other goddesses, she lost her cosmic power. In the first dynasty she was recognized as the source, the seat of divine and royal power. Her hieroglyph is a throne; in reliefs and sculptures she is most often shown wearing the throne on her head. It is the throne that makes the king, king. He is Horus; she is his mother. A later myth tries to show that Isis originally received her power from Re, the ruler of the world, through trickery. In the tale Isis is Re's granddaughter. One day when he is old and weary, with tottering limbs and dribbling lips, she sets a poisonous scorpion whose sting only she can heal in his path. As price of his cure, she extorts from him the secret name which puts him in her power.

Her power was that of an enchantress. The throne symbol misleads, for Isis was originally not a political but a nature goddess, identified with the annually renewed rise of the Nile. She represented the feminine creative power which conceived every living creature. Her nurturing love pervaded both earth and afterworld. As descendent of the prehistoric bird goddess, she often wore a vulture headdress and bore the vulture's wide-spreading protecting wings. She carried a papyrus sceptre in her hand and horns and the solar disc on her head.

Of course Isis is most fully revealed in the long complex tale about her brother-spouse Osiris's murder, her rememberment and revival of his corpse, the conception and birth of their son Horus, and her support of the youthful Horus's heroic struggles to recapture the throne from his usurpatious uncle, Set. The myth is too elaborate and too familiar to retell in detail here, but it shows her as goddess of fertility and regeneration, of mourning and all underworld experience. Like many others I find especially moving the account of Isis going from nome to nome to gather up the fourteen scattered parts of Osiris's body, and the image of her hovering over her husband's immobile corpse and gently, persistently, flapping those lovely wings until slowly, slowly his penis arises and becomes erect and she lowers herself onto it. The reliefs at Abydos are also beautiful: the series of pictures which show the lovely winged goddess with the pharoah's head tucked between her chin and shoulder, with the pharoah nursing at her breast, and sitting, wing-enfolded, on her lap.

Yet of all the Egyptian goddesses, the one by whom I have been most deeply stirred is Hathor, both in her primary manifestation as goddess of love and beauty, and in her Sekhmet aspect, as goddess of destruction. Clearly a predynastic divinity, she was later identified with every important local goddess and associated with all the major national ones: Mut, Bast, Sekhmet, and Isis. Her shrines were even more numerous than those of Horus, the other truly ancient divinity with whom she is so often paired.

The female counterpart of Re, she was a primary creatrix who was perpetually conceiving, creating, and rearing. She was the mother of her father—and of every god and goddess. Goddess of love and pleasure, of beauty and art, of the vine and of joy, she was the rise of the Nile and the beautifully sounding sistrum. Above all, she was the nurturant wild cow and most often represented as a cow or as a lovely woman with the ears and horns of the cow. Perhaps these horns signify the same miraculously fast-growing regenerative powers associated with the horns of the bull in Old Europe, but here they encircled not the lunar but the solar disk—as though the masculine and feminine symbolic elements had been reversed.

Hathor was preeminently a goddess of women. Although nurse to every pharoah, she was particularly important to Hatshepsut. Among the most beautiful representations of divine nurturance I have found anywhere is the relief in Hatshepsut's temple at Thebes which shows the female pharaoh on her knees below the belly of the cow goddess, sucking at the ripe full udder. Hathor was a goddess of childbirth and also the goddess who offered her milk-filled breasts to the newly dead and tenderly carried them on her back. In the Late Period the deceased were called Hathor not Osiris.

In one of her aspects she was known as Sekhmet, the Powerful, and as Sekhmet she is terrifying. A daughter of Re, the sun god, Sekhmet was identified with the scorching power of the noonday sun and most commonly represented as a lionheaded humanlike female, though she also appeared as a crocodile. She was known as the Eye of Re and as defender of the divine order. She was placed as the uraeus serpent on Re's brow and was also herself depicted as wearing the solar disk and the uraeus (which symbolized the power that rules the world). As Re's Eye, Sekhmet was also the creatrix. According to one of the many Egyptian creation myths, humans grew from the tears shed by Re's eye when, having gone off on her own, she was forced to return. Thus from the beginning Sekhmet is associated with the tragic dimension of human existence.

As fearsome maintainer of order, Sekhmet was regarded as the punisher of the damned in the underworld. Though paired with both Ptah and Atum, she was never viewed as a subordinated spouse. Sekhmet was associated with Bast, the mild cat-faced goddess who personifies the fertilizing warmth of the sun and with Mut, consort of Atum, at Karnak. Adjoining the Atum-dedicated temple complex at Karnak is a Temple to Mut where archaeologists have found 365 statues of Sekhmet, each subtly different, indicating her dominion over every day of the year. Though a goddess in her own right, she was also seen as a manifestation of Hathor, the goddess of love, pleasure, and beauty. Hathor was most often revered as a benevolent goddess who gives support and nourishment to living humans who suck at her breasts and to the newly dead as they arrive in the underworld—but as Sekhmet she was terrifying.

The most powerful Egyptian myth I know is one that involves Hathor in her Sekhmet aspect. The Egyptian gods who will someday die were also, of course, susceptible to aging as their Greek counterparts never were. In this particular story Re has become an old man, incontinent, dribbling from his mouth, senile, and impotent. When the humans become aware of his weakness and begin to plot against him, Re sends out his Eye in the shape of his lioness daughter to subdue the rebellion. Although initially Sekhmet sets about her destructive work in order to restore balance, she soon gets carried way with her own bloodthirsti-ness. "When I slay men, my heart rejoices," she proclaims. Having tasted blood, she will not be appeased. She seems prepared to annihi-late all humankind. But Re had meant only to uphold the divine order, to restore the balance between gods and humans, and knows that somehow his daughter must be stopped. The gods in concert come up with a solution. They fill the battlefield with several thousand urns of beer mixed with pomegranate juice. Greedily Sekhmet swallows the contents of the first vessel. "Ahah, more blood," she gloats, as she empties urn after urn, until finally she falls asleep in a drunken stupor. When she awakes, she has come back to her senses, to her more Hathor-like nature.

When modern commentators speak of Sekhmet as an evilly destruc-tive goddess, they seem to forget that "the gods of Egypt can be terrify-ing, dangerous, and unpredictable, but they cannot be evil. . . . All are necessary features of the existent world and of the limited disorder that is essential to a living order. "[17] When I remember the facial expression on the many ancient statues of Sekhmet that I have seen—at Luxor, in the museums of Cairo, New York, and Europe—I perceive not evil but an acceptance of the death-bringing energy that sometimes possesses her as integral to her nature. I see a look of weary compassion, the look of someone who sees the irreducible tragedy of life which she can do nothing to avert and which, indeed, she knows she has herself helped bring about—but who does not hide from the pain. I recall also the attitude toward her of her contemporary Egyptian attendants. At Karnak the guards assume that to be taken to the dark locked shrine in which stands a perfectly preserved statue of a regal Sekhmet is the most valuable perquisite they can offer a visitor. At the Temple of Mut the guards show enormous reluctance to share their goddess with anyone not likely to share their devotion. At both sites I was moved by the love, not just awe, that these attendants feel for her and by the sensuous appreciation with which they stroke her breasts. Clearly they know her as a source of blessing and not only of destruction.

I find in the myth about Sekhmet's rampage a powerful reminder of the importance of coming to terms with destructive energy. The dark side of the Greek goddesses is comparatively so muted, so human in scale, so much easier to acknowledge and integrate. Sekhmet reminds us that there are darker energies—in us, as humans, as natural beings. She helps us recognize these energies are natural ones —not pure evil or satanic, but part of a whole—as Sekhmet is an aspect of Hathor. I see us, us humans, as like her with our initially creative energies so fearfully out of hand. And I mourn what we may do.

The only poem I know which hints at the recognition that the energies which produced the atom bomb are our creative energies, are expressions of eros and not only of death longing, is William Carlos Williams's "Asphodel, That Greeny Flower":

> *The bomb puts an end*
> *to all that.*
> *I am reminded*
> *that the bomb*
> *also*
> *is a flower*
> *dedicated*
> *howbeit*
> *to our destruction.*
> *The mere picture*
> *of the exploding bomb*
> *fascinates us*
> *so that we cannot wait*
> *to prostrate ourselves*
> *before it. We do not believe*
> *that love*
> *can so wreck our lives.* [18]

The Egyptians knew that everything eventually comes to an end—even the gods, even the *ba* that survives the death of the body. For them endlessness was itself death, nonexistence. Yet they also loved life, ordinary daily life in this world—loved it so passionately that they did everything they could to extend it, even after death. The tombs, the funerary temples, the elaborate death cult, all mark a celebration of *life*. Nowhere is this more evident than at Abydos. Even now the temple of Osiris standing there invites us to share in that love of life and that acceptance of death.

The exposure to Egyptian mythology has taught me that accepting that we as a species may die means celebrating the beauty of our every-day life here, living it as fully and creatively and gratefully as we are able. I remember Atum telling Osiris that after all the familiar world is destroyed he will still remain. I think I understand what that means.

I feel I understand exactly why Christa Wolf included in her essays not just the conclusions of her thinking but its contexts, the bread she had just finished baking, the apple tree outside her window, the conversations with her husband. My vision is not apocalyptic. I do not see our probable end as punishment. I do not see our present world as ugly or evil. I delight in my sunset walks on the beach. I get deeply and passionately involved in my teaching and writing. I rejoice in the birth of my grandchildren. I keep remembering the answer given by that young German to my intense questioning about how I might most meaningfully live my life—by showing that it is still possible to live an ordinary life.

And having seen the Peace Garden at Nagasaki in bloom where it was said nothing would grow for a century, having seen the moss reappear almost miraculously at Mount St. Helens within a year of the volcano's eruption, I have a deep and to me comforting assurance that there will still be life, even if no longer human life, on this beautiful planet that has been our home, no matter what we may do. What the Egyptians recognized as *there*, transcendent to us, will still persist—albeit changed, in forms we might not recognize.

To celebrate life, the Egyptians knew, means not holding on to the forms of it immediately given. I bless what I have learned from those who lived near the beginning that helps me to understand what it is like to live near what may be the ending. In such a time I want to say: We, you and I, are beautiful and worthy of love. Let us remember to honor that worthiness while we are here to do so.

Notes

1. INITIATION

An earlier version of this chapter appeared in *American Poetry Review,* July/August 1976.

1. Cf. especially C. G. Jung, "Woman in Europe," *Collected Works* (Princeton: Princeton University Press, 1953–79), 10:113–133 (hereafter cited as *CW*).
2. Irene Claremont de Castillejo, "Soul Images of Women," *Knowing Woman* (New York: Harper & Row, 1973), 165–82.
3. James Hillman, *Anima: The Anatomy of a Personified Notion* (Dallas: Spring Publications, 1985), 5–16.
4. M. Esther Harding, *Woman's Mysteries* (New York: Bantam, 1973), 11.
5. Ibid., 20.
6. Ibid., 42.
7. Ibid., 162.
8. Ibid., 20.
9. Ibid., 85.
10. Ibid., 89.
11. Ibid., 133, 134.
12. Ibid., 121, 122, 123.

2. RITES OF INCORPORATION

1. Helene Cixioux, "Sorties," in Helene Cixioux and Catherine Clement, *The Newly Born Woman* (Minneapolis: University of Minnesota Press, 1986), 63–64. My thanks to Suzanne Harding for reminding me of this litany.
2. Rainer Maria Rilke, *Letters to a Young Poet* (New York: Random House, 1984), 77–78.
3. Judith Butler, *Gender Trouble* (New York: Routledge, 1990), 13.
4. Elizabeth V. Spelman, *Inessential Woman: Problems of Exclusion in Feminist Thought* (Boston: Beacon Press, 1988), 3.

5. Luce Irigaray, *This Sex Which Is Not One* (Ithaca, N. Y.: Cornell University Press, 1985), 134.

6. Diana Fuss, *Essentially Speaking* (New York: Routledge, 1989), 36.

7. Marge Piercy, "Unlearning to Not Speak," *Circles on the Water* (New York: Alfred A. Knopf, 1982), 97.

8. Donna Wilshire, "The Uses of Myth, Image, and the Female Body in Revisioning Knowledge," in Alison M. Jagar and Susan Bordo, eds., *Gender/ Body/Knowledge:Feminist Reconstructions of Being and Knowing* (New Brunswick, N. J.: Rutgers University Press, 1989), 92.

9. Dorothy Dinnerstein, *The Mermaid and the Minotaur* (New York: Harper & Row, 1977), 202–5.

10. Ernst Pfeiffer, ed., *Sigmund Freud and Lou Andreas Salome: Letters* (New York: Harcourt Brace Jovanovich, 1966), 208.

11. Robert Hughes, "The Art of Frank Auerbach," *New York Times Magazine,* 11 October 1990, 23.

12. Butler, *Gender Trouble,* 64.

13. Ibid., 24.

14. Ibid., 6.

15. Ibid., 113.

16. Muriel Rukeyser, "Myth," *Out of Silence* (New York: Tri-Quarterly Press, 1992), 20.

17. Adrienne Rich, "Transcendental Etude," *Dream of a Common Language* (New York: W. W. Norton, 1978), 75.

18. Butler, *Gender Trouble,* 119.

19. Ibid., 16.

20. Luce Irigaray, *Speculum of the Other Woman* (Ithaca, N. Y.: Cornell University Press, 1985), 11.

21. James Hillman, *Healing Fictions* (Barrytown, N. Y.: Station Hill Press, 1983), 113.

3. RITES OF EXORCISM

1. Mary Daly, *Webster's First New Intergalactic Wickedary of the English Language* (Boston: Beacon Press, 1987), 75.

2. Sheila Greeve Davaney, "Problems with Feminist Theory: Historicity and the Search for Sure Foundations," in Paula M. Cooey, Sharon A. Farmer, and Mary Ellen Ross, eds., *Embodied Love* (San Francisco: Harper & Row, 1987), 85.

3. Rosemary Ruether, *Sexism and God-Talk* (Boston: Beacon Press, 1983), 22.

4. Edward Glover, *Freud or Jung?* (New York: Meridian, 1956), is wittily but mischievously unfair to Jung; Philip Rieff's commitment to Freud's therapeutic skepticism (*The Triumph of the Therapeutic* [New York: Harper & Row, 1966]) leads him to disparage Jung for pandering to our longings for salvation; Norman O. Brown (*Life Against Death* [New York: Random House, 1959]) seems

to need to protect his own "overcoming" of Freud from contamination by Jung's influence almost as assiduously as Freud guarded himself from Nietzsche's influence. Jungians tend to take over uncritically Jung's pejorative version of Freud. Even Lillian Frey-Rohn, whose *From Freud to Jung* (New York: Dell, 1974) shows she has read Freud's own works with care, perpetuates the vision of Freud as promulgator of a reductive, mechanistic, pathology-focused psychology which cast a spell on Jung and temporarily blocked his discovery of "the vital; and nourishing aspects of the depths of the psyche."

5. Paul Roazen, *Freud and His Followers* (New York: New American Library, 1974), 276–79.

6. Pfeiffer, ed., *Sigmund Freud and Lou Andreas Salome* (see chap. 2, n. 10. above), 133.

7. Gaston Bachelard, *The Poetics of Reverie* (Boston: Beacon Press, 1971), 97–142.

8. Cf. Demaris S.Wehr, "Religious and Social Dimensions of Jung's Concept of the Anima," in Estella Lauter and Carol Schreier Rupprecht, eds., *Feminist Archetypal Theory* (Knoxville: University of Tennessee Press, 1985), 27.

9. Jung, "The Relations between the Ego and the Unconscious," *CW* 8: 190.

10. Jung, "The Structure of the Unconscious," *CW* 8: 286, 289.

11. James Hillman, *ReVisioning Psychology* (New York: Harper & Row, 1975), 158.

12. Jung, "Archetypes of the Collective Unconscious." *CW* 9: 31.

13. Ellenberger, *The Discovery of the Unconscious* (New York: Basic Books, 1970), 480–84.

14. Evelyn Fox Keller's *Reflections on Science and Gender* (New Haven: Yale University Press, 1985) shows the prevalence of this gendered rhetoric in the history of the physical and natural sciences; Susan Griffin's more poetically intense *Women and Nature* (New York: Harper & Row, 1978) expresses the painful consequences.

15. Cf. Demaris Wehr, "Uses and Abuses of Jung's Psychology of Women: Animus," *Anima* 12, no.1 (Fall 1985): 13–23.

16. Jung, "Psychology of the Transference," *CW* 16: 245.

17. Celia Bertin, *Marie Bonaparte: A Life* (San Diego: Harcourt Brace Jovanovich, 1981); Helene Deutsch, *Confrontations with Myself* (New York: W. W. Norton, 1975): Paul Roazen, *Helene Deutsch: A Psychoanalyst's Life* (New York: New American Library, 1985).

18. Karen Horney, *Feminine Psychology* (New York: W. W. Norton, 1967).

19. Clara Thompson, *On Women* (New York: New American Library, 1971).

20. The most readily accessible version of Wolf's typology to English readers is to be found in Ann Belford Ulanov, *The Feminine in Jungian Psychology and in Christian Theology* (Chicago: Northwestern University Press, 1973).

21. Emma Jung, *Anima and Animus* (Zurich: Spring Publications, 1974).

22. Marie Louise von Franz, *A Psychological Interpretation of the Golden Ass of Apuleius* (Dallas: Spring Publications, 1980).

23. Castillejo, "Soul Images" (see chap. 1, n. 2 above).

24. Kate Millett, "Freud and the Influence of Psychoanalytic Thought," *Sexual Politics* (Garden City, N. Y.: Doubleday, 1970).

25. Juliet Mitchell, *Psychoanalysis and Feminism* (New York: Pantheon, 1974).

26. Naomi Goldenberg, "A Feminist Critique of Jung," *Signs* 2, no. 2 (Winter 1976): 443–49.

27. Carol Gilligan, *In a Different Voice* (Cambridge: Harvard University Press, 1982).

28. Nancy Chodorov, *The Reproduction of Mothering* (Berkeley: University of California Press, 1978); Dorothy Dinnerstein, *The Mermaid and the Minotaur* (New York: Harper & Row, 1977).

29. Butler, *Gender Trouble* (see chap. 2, n. 3 above), 19.

30. Fuss, *Essentially Speaking* (see chap. 2, n. 6 above), 48.

31. Rilke, *Letters to a Young Poet* (see chap. 2, n. 2 above), 41.

32. Otto Rank, *Beyond Psychology* (New York: Dover, 1941). I find it interesting that this book of Rank's dates from the same year (the year both died) as Freud's "Analysis Terminable and Interminable" in which the latter emphasizes the importance for all humans of getting past the "repudiation of the feminine," of vulnerability and passivity, which he sees as blocking us from coming to terms with human limitation and mortality, and thus with human life.

33. Rank, *Beyond Psychology*, 290, 242, 243.

4. BODY AND SOUL

1. William Chase Greene, *Moira: Fate, Good, and Evil in Greek Thought* (New York: Harper & Row, 1963), 23, 146 and *passim*.

2. R. B. Onions, *The Origins of European Thought* (Cambridge: Cambridge University Press, 1989), 405.

3. Hesiod, *Theogony*, lines 904, 217.

4. Onions, *Origins*, 391.

5. Homer, *Odyssesy*, 1:32–34.

6. Paul Tillich, "Philosophy and Fate," *The Protestant Era* (Chicago: University of Chicago Press, 1963), 4. I think Richard Underwood for reminding me of this essay and suggesting its relevance to my purposes here. Unfortunately, the published English version, as the English title suggests, consistently renders *Schicksal* as "fate," and thus occludes my point, even though the translator notes that the German word "combines the meaning of 'fate' and 'destiny.'" But *Schicksal*, which derives from *schicken*, "to send," like "destiny" clearly connotes the teleological vector. Though characters in nineteenth-century German novels may often bemoan their *Schicksal* as though it was their predetermined fate, the context makes clear that this communicates their desire to evade their own responsibility and to deny their complicity in what happens to them. I have therefore substituted "destiny" in my quotations from the essay —which conforms to the decisions of Freud's translators. I thank Eric Downing for these suggestions about the German.

7. Sigmund Freud, *The Standard Edition of the Complete Psychological Works of Sigmund Freud* (London: Hogarth Press, 1933–74), 11:189 (hereafter cited as *SE*).

8. Freud, *SE* 19:178. Although the phrase occurs in a section of the essay where Freud is still speaking of the little girl's discovery of the "inferiority" of her clitoris in comparison to a male playmate's penis and her consequent acceptance of "castration as an accomplished fact"; that is, in this transitional essay, Freud is here still speaking of female anatomy in terms of male genitalia.

9. Ernst Jones, "The Early Development of Female Sexuality" and "Early Female Sexuality," *Papers on Psychoanalysis* (Baltimore, Md.: Williams & Wilkins, 1948), 438–51, 485–95.

10. Horney, "The Flight from Womanhood" (see chap. 3, n. 18 above), . 54–70.

11. Helene Deustch, "The Psychology of Women in Relation to Reproduction," in Jean Strouse, ed., *Women and Analysis* (New York: Grossman Publishers, 1974), 147–61.

12. Letter to Carl Muller-Braunschweig, 21 July 1935, in Donald L. Burnham, "Freud and Female Sexuality: A Previously Unpublished Letter," *Psychiatry* 34 (August 1971): 329.

13. Naomi Goldenberg, *Returning Words to Flesh* (Boston: Beacon Press, 1990), 177.

14. As suggested by Thomas Laquer, *Making Sex: Body and Gender from the Greeks to Freud* (Cambridge: Harvard University Press, 1990), 25.

15. Jane Gallop, *Thinking Through the Body* (New York: Columbia University Press, 1988), 125, 8.

16. Goldenberg, *Returning Words,* 181.

17. Adrienne Rich, *Of Woman Born* (New York: Bantam, 1977), 290

18. Gallop, *Thinking,* 1, 3, 4.

19. Adrienne Rich, *Blood, Bread, and Poetry* (New York: W. W. Norton, 1986), 215.

20. Jeni Couzyn, "The Way Toward Each Other," *Life by Drowning* (Newcastle upon Tyne: Bloodaxe Press, 1985), 141.

21. Gallop, *Thinking,* 13.

22. Kim Chernin, in Kim Chernin and Renate Stendhal, *Sex and Other Sacred Games* (New York: Times Books, 1989), 36

23. Alma Luz Villanueva, "Sisters," *Bloodroot* (Place of Herons Press: San Antonio, Tex., 1977).

24. Marianne Hirsch, *The Mother/Daughter Plot* (Bloomington: Indiana University Press, 1989).

25. Rosemary J. Dudley, "She Who Bleeds Yet Does Not Die," *Heresies: The Great Goddess Issue*, Spring 1978, 113, 114.

26. Judy Grahn, "From Sacred Blood to the Curse and Beyond," in Charlene Spretnak, ed., *The Politics of Women's Spirituality* (Garden City, N. Y.: Anchor Books, 1982), 268.

27. Cf. Thomas Buckley and Almas Gottlieb, eds., *Blood Magic: The Anthropology of Menstruation* (Berkeley: University of California Press, 1988).

28. Grahn, "Sacred Blood," 272.

29. Cf. Merida Wexler, "The Menstrual Hut," privately printed brochure.

30. Sharon Olds, "The Moment," *The Dead and the Living* (New York: Alfred A, Knopf, 1983), 42.

31. Marge Piercy, "Something to Look Forward To," in *Available Light* (New York: Middlemarch, 1988), 86.

32. Emily Martin, "Premenstrual Syndrome: Work and Anger in Late Industrial Society," in Buckley and Gottlieb, *Blood Magic,* 174.

33. Copied out long ago from an advertisement in the *New York Review of Books.*

34. Janice Delaney, Mary Long Lupton, and Emily Toth, eds., *The Curse: A Cultural History of Menstruation* (Urbana: University of Illinois Press, 1988), 279.

35. Excerpts from these letters by Merida Wexler are included with her permission; my grateful thanks.

36. Kathee Miller, "Mysteries," *Venus Rising* 2, no. 6 (sept./Oct. 1988), unpaginated.

37. Again, my thanks to Merida Wexler.

38. Wexler, used with permission.

39. Freud, "The Taboo of Virginity," *SE* 12:193–208.

40. Giulia Sassa, *Greek Virginity* (Cambridge: Harvard University Press, 1990).

41. Cf. the chapter on Hera in my *The Goddess* (New York: Crossroad, 1981). I find it fascinating how these images get turned upside down and back around! I think, for instance, of "nymphomania," a term which illustrates perfectly the "blame the victim" scenario. In Greek mythology the nymphs are dedicated virgins, who in tale after tale are raped or seduced by males, or die trying to escape from them. One such nymph, Eos, who succeeded in evading her pursuer, was then as punishment condemned to be incessantly infatuated with men. Somehow she then becomes the very model of nymphic sexuality!

42. E. M. Broner, *A Weave of Women* (New York: Bantam, 1982), chap. 3.

43. Diane Wolkstein and Samuel Noah Kramer, *Inanna* (New York: Harper & Row, 1983), 37, 44.

44. Stendhal, in Chernin and Stendahl, *Sacred Games,* 246.

45. Shere Hite, *The Hite Report* (New York: Dell, 1976); cf. the fine discussion in Gallop, *Thinking,* 70-88.

46. Gallop, *Thinking*, 75.

47. Ibid., 108.

48. Ibid., 82

49. Jan Zita Grover, "Words to Lust By," *Women's Review of Books* 7 (November 1990): 23.

50. Stendhal, in Chernin and Stendhal, *Sacred Games,* 237.

51. Grover, "Words," 21.

52. Freud, "Analysis Terminable and Interminable," *SE* 23:253–544.

53. Iragaray, *This Sex* (see chap. 2, n. 5 above), 63, 64.

54. Gallop, *Thinking,* 94.

55. Chernin, in Chernin and Stendhal, *Sacred Games,* 101.

56. Gallop, *Thinking,* 1100.

57. Stendhal, in Chernin and Stendhal, *Sacred Games,* 221–22.

58. Merida Wexler, letter, used with permission.

59. Cf. particularly Freud, "The Theme of the Three Caskets," *SE* 12:291–302; "The 'Uncanny,' "*SE* 17:219–52.

60. "An Indian pregnancy song lamenting the fate of being a woman," included in Verrier Elwin and Shamroa Hivale, eds., *Folksongs of the Maikal Hills* (London: Oxford University Press, 1944), 246; my thanks to Penelope Washbourn for including this lament in her *Seasons of Woman* (San Francisco: Harper & Row, 1979), 87.

61. Judith Walzer Leavitt, *Brought to Bed: Childbearing in America, 1770–1950* (New York: Oxford University Press, 1986).

62. Jean Thomson, "What Freud Offers Toward Understanding the Psychical Reality of Infertility in Women: An Introduction," 11; used with permission of author.

63. Ibid., *passim.*

64. Miller, "Mysteries."

65. Elieen Moeller, "ten years ago," in Marilyn Sewell, ed., *Cries of the Spirit: A Celebration of Women's Spirituality* (Boston: Beacon Press, 1991), 104.

66. Lucille Clifton, "The Lost Baby Poem," *Good News About the Earth* (New York: Random House, 1972), 4.

67. Once again my thanks to Merida Wexler.

68. Alta Gerry, "3:6," *The Shameless Hussy* (Trumansburg, N.Y.: Crossing Press).

69. Cf. Marija Gimbutas, *The Language of the Goddess* (San Francisco: Harper & Row, 1989).

70. Sara Ruddick, *Maternal Thinking* (Boston: Beacon Press, 1989), 72.

71. Ibid., *passim.*

72. May Sarton, "Now I Become Myself," *Collected Poems: 1930–1973* (New York: W. W. Norton, 1974), 156.

73. Carol Christ, "Reverence for Life: The Need for a Sense of Finitude," in Cooey et al., *Embodied Love* (see chap. 3, n. 2 above), 52.

5. RITES OF ANCIENT RIPENING

A slightly different version of this chapter appeared in *Anima* 17, no. 2 (Spring 1991).

1. For a full account of this dream, cf. Christine Downing, *Journey Through Menopause* (New York: Crossroad, 1989), 45–47.

2. Cf. Christine Downing, *Psyche's Sisters* (San Francisco: Harper & Row, 1988), 3.

3. Thomas M. Falkner, "Homeric Heroism, Old Age, and the End of the

Odyssey," in Thomas M. Falkner and Judith de Luce, *Old Age in Greek and Latin Literature* (Albany: State University of New York Press, 1989), 33.

4. James Hillman, *Puer Papers* (Irving, Tex.: Spring Publications, 1979), 15-23.

5. Cf. Mary Daly, *Gyn/Ecology* (Boston: Beacon Press, 1979), 16, 427; Barbara G. Walker, *The Crone: Woman of Age, Wisdom, and Power* (San Francisco: Harper & Row, 1985), *passim*.

6. Daly, *Webster's First . . . Wickedary* (see chap. 3, n. 1 above), 114–16; Walker, *The Crone*, 31.

7. Laurel Rust, "Another Part of the Country," *Women and Aging, Calyx* 9:2 and 3 (Winter 1988): 137.

8. Sandra Scofield, Review of Charlotte Painter's *Gifts of Age, Women and Aging*, 210

9. May Sarton, *At Seventy* (New York: W. W. Norton, 1984), 37.

10. Downing, *Menopause*, 17.

11. Sarton, *Seventy*, 136.

12. Baba Copper, "Voices: On Becoming Old Women," *Women and Aging*, 56.

13. Shevy Healey, "Growing to Be an Old Woman," *Women and Aging*, 61.

14. Sarton, *Seventy*, 10.

15. Adrienne Rich, *Your Native Land, Your Life* (New York: W. W. Norton, 1986), 100.

16. Audre Lorde, *A Burst of Light*, (Ithaca, N. Y.: Firebrand Books, 1988), 79, 85.

17. Rich, *Native Land*, 98.

18. Copper, "Voices," 47–48.

19. Healey, "Growing," 58.

20. James Hillman, "The Feeling Function," in Marie-Louise von Franz and James Hillman, *Lectures on Jung's Typology*, (Irving, Tex.: Spring Publications, 1979), 113–14.

21. Barbara Macdonald, "Outside the Sisterhood," *Women and Aging*, 23, 24, 22.

22. Barbara Macdonald, in Macdonald and Cynthia Rich, *Look Me in the Eye* (San Francisco: Spinsters, Ink, 1983), 58, 21, 80.

23. Healey, "Growing," 61.

24. Helen M. Luke, *Old Age* (New York: Parabola Books, 1987), 92–94.

25. Healey, "Growing," 60.

26. Macdonald, in Macdonald and Rich, *Look*, 19.

27. Luke, *Old Age*, 92–93.

28. Eleanor Garner, "The Challenge of Aging: A Woman's View" (talk given to the San Diego Friends of Jung, 11 May 1988). Typescript copyright by Eleanor P. Garner, used with permission.

29. Luke, *Old Age*, 70.

30. Macdonald, in Macdonald and Rich, *Look*, 114–15.

31. Copper, "Voices," 55.

32. Healey, "Growing," 62.

33. Walker, *The Crone*, 17, 19, 33, 86.

34. Ibid., 37, 74.

35. Macdonald, in Macdonald and Rich, *Look*, 99.

36. Lorde, *Light*, 130, 124, 131.

37. Ibid., 119, 118.

38. Carolyn G. Heilbrun, *Writing a Woman's Life* (New York: W.W. Norton, 1988), 130.

39. Sarton, *Seventy*, 10.

40. Cf. Wolkstein and Kramer, *Inanna* (see chap. 4, n. 43 above), 51.

41. Luke, *Old Age*, 44, 63, 60.

42. Ibid., 73, 72, 75.

43. Florida Scott-Maxwell, *The Measure of My Days* (New York: Penguin, 1988), 5, 138, 89, 32.

44. Ibid., 13, 131.

45. Luke, *Old Age*, 69, 104, 95, 106, 110.

46. Lorde, *Light*, 114, 111.

47. Scott-Maxwell, *Measure*, 19.

48. Luke, *Old Age*, 94–5.

49. Scott-Maxwell, *Measure*, 41.

50. Ibid., 142.

51. Elsa Gidlow, *Elsa: I Come With My Songs* (San Francisco: Booklegger Press, 1986), 391.

52. Macdonald, in Macdonald and Rich, *Look*, 75.

53. Meridel LeSueur, *Ripening* (Old Westbury, N.Y.: The Feminist Press, 1982), 263.

6. EVEN THE GODS WILL DIE

Earlier versions of parts of this chapter appeared in *Soundings*, Fall 1985, and *Anima*, Fall 1987.

1. Frederich Hölderlin, "Bread and Wine," translated by Douglas Scott, in Martin Heidegger, *Existence and Being* (Chicago: Henry Regnery, 1949), 291.

2. Christa Wolf, *Cassandra* (New York: Farrar, Straus and Giroux, 1984), 180, 232.

3. Ibid., 260.

4. Ibid., 283, 251.

5. Eugenio Montale, *Otherwise* (New York: Random House, 1984), 13.

6. Dinnerstein, *The Mermaid* (see chap. 2, n. 9 above), 209.

7. Marija Gimbutas, *The Gods and Goddesses of Old Europe* (Berkeley and Los Angeles: University of California Press, 1982), 197.

8. C. G. Jung, *Memories, Dreams, Relections* (New York: Pantheon Books, 1963), 158–60.

9. Rainer Maria Rilke, posthumously published poem quoted in Erik Hornung, *Conceptions of God in Ancient Egypt* (London: Routledge & Kegan Paul, 1983), 17.

10. E. A. Wallis Budge, *The Gods of the Egyptians* (New York: Dover Publications, 1969), 334.

11. Hornung, *Conceptions of God*, 185.

12. Denise Levertov, "Beginners," *Candles in Babylon* (New York: New Directions, 1982).

13. Rainer Maria Rilke, *Duino Elegies and the Sonnets to Orpheus*, trans. A. Poulin, Jr. (Boston: Houghton Mifflin, 1977), 55.

14. Hornung, *Conceptions of God*, 157.

15. Ibid., 163.

16. Friedrich Nietzsche, *The Birth of Tragedy.* (New York: Doubleday/Anchor, 1956), 30.

17. Hornung *Conceptions of God,*, 213.

18. William Carlos Williams, "Asphodel, That Greeny Flower," *The Collected Poems of William Carlos Williams, Vol. II, 1939–1962* (New York: New Directions, 1988), 321–22.

Index